Fashion Collections

Edited by
Nicola Misani
Paola Varacca Capello
Foreword by Marco Bizzarri

BUP

Product Development
and Merchandising

Original Title: Le collezioni nella moda
Copyright © 2016 EGEA S.p.A.

Translation: Andrew Spannaus for Language Solutions for Business
Typesetting: Laura Panigara, Cesano Boscone (MI)

Copyright © 2017 Bocconi University Press
EGEA S.p.A.

EGEA S.p.A.
Via Salasco, 5 - 20136 Milano
Tel. 02/5836.5751 – Fax 02/5836.5753
egea.edizioni@unibocconi.it – www.egeaeditore.it

All rights reserved, including but not limited to translation, total or partial adaptation, reproduction, and communication to the public by any means on any media (including microfilms, films, photocopies, electronic or digital media), as well as electronic information storage and retrieval systems. For more information or permission to use material from this text, see the website www.egeaeditore.it

Given the characteristics of Internet, the publisher is not responsible for any changes of address and contents of the websites mentioned.

First Edition: February 2017

ISBN International Edition 978-88-85486-21-8
ISBN Domestic Edition 978-88-99902-14-8
ISBN Mobypocket Edition 978-88-85486-23-2
ISBN Epub Edition 978-88-85486-22-5

Print: Digital Print Service, Segrate (MI)

Table of Contents

Foreword, by *Marco Bizzarri* — VII

Introduction, by *Nicola Misani and Paola Varacca Capello* — 1

1 The Recent Evolution of Fashion
by *Nicola Misani and Paola Varacca Capello* — 5
 1 Fashion: products, style and innovation — 5
 2 How fashion is born, and how it evolves — 9
 3 The changes in the system — 12
 4 Sustainability in fashion — 15
 5 Impacts on collection development — 19

2 The Variety of Companies and Collection Development
by *Davide Ravasi and Paola Varacca Capello* — 25
 1 Criteria for classifying companies — 25
 2 The logic of interaction with the market — 30
 3 The style/industry relationship — 36
 4 Organizational roles — 45
 5 The rational or relational approach to collection development — 47

3 Collections and the Development Process
by *Flavio Sciuccati and Paola Varacca Capello* — 51
 1 The fundamental elements of collections — 51
 2 Timing and activities (collection timing) — 58
 3 Activities in the collection development process — 63

4 Fashion Trends
by *Diego Rinallo* — 75
 1 Fashion trends and collection development — 75

2	The actors (i): trend producers and hunters	77
3	The actors (ii): media, retailers and celebrities	81
4	Trend geography	84
5	Social media and the new role of consumers in spreading trends	85

5 Market Analysis and the Formulation of Guidelines
by *Giorgio Brandazza and Paola Varacca Capello* 91

1	The definition of collection guidelines	91
2	Analysis of sales data	95
3	ABC analysis	99
4	Some examples of data analysis and processing and definition of guidelines	101

6 The Balance between Creativity and Rationality in Collection Development: the Merchandising Plan
by *Giorgio Brandazza and Paola Varacca Capello* 111

1	The merchandising plan: content and methodology	111
2	The process and the main problems in building the plan	115
3	The role of the merchandiser	120
4	The merchandising tool	124

7 The Activities of the Collection Development Process and their Critical Aspects
by *Flavio Sciuccati and Paola Varacca Capello* 129

1	Managing complexity: planning	129
2	Managing complexity: industrialization	136
3	Managing complexity: the reduction of variety	139

The Authors 151

Foreword

by *Marco Bizzarri*

I was pleased to accept the invitation to write the preface for this book for a number of reasons. First and foremost, I feel passionate about the topic. I then thought about a presentation I made to the students of the Bocconi University in September 2015, nine months after having assumed my position as CEO of Gucci. On that occasion, I told the story of the journey I have taken in my career, the choices I have made, the obstacles I have overcome and the lessons I have learned along the way. Experiences that help to shape you for your next challenge. In taking on the role at Gucci, I drew upon all my past experiences as I set about reinvigorating the company, which given its size and complexity and the expectation for fast results was not straightforward.

Probably the most fundamental and unique factor that determines success in our sector is the need for a perfect harmony between the creative and business competencies. Neither should ever be sacrificed at the expense of the other.

As the CEO of a fashion company you know that you have to establish conditions that nurture creative talents, who have great sensitivity towards products, developed over the course of years of study, work, experience, and through their personal lives. These individuals have a skill that you do not have. Your job is to open up possibilities for them and ensure they realize that the company will do everything to bring their creative vision to life. The biggest mistake you can make as a manager is to think that you should constrain and shape them.

This means understanding how they work, what they fear, what they love, what they detest, and make sure that the team and the entire company allow them to do what they know how to do. Their ideas must flourish. Their talent must be expressed.

Therefore, my first principle of management today is the importance of creating an environment of empowerment and respect. It is of course necessary to respect not only the company's creative director, who has such a pivotal role, but all of the employees of the company. In fact, on arriving at Gucci, the first thing I did was to meet as many colleagues in the company as I could, in all of the functions and markets. Considering that the only evident and concrete signs of the new Gucci were two fashion shows, in January and February 2015, while everything else - stores, products, website, advertising campaigns - did not yet express the new Gucci we were envisioning. It was essential for me to meet and talk to as many colleagues as possible to explain the new vision and identity we wanted to give the brand. I calculated that I met three thousand people on those trips. I shook everyone's hand.

I presented the new strategy and told them what I expected from them. I explained that there would be significant changes and that there would be risks which they would be empowered to take. It meant that the company would accept the fact that mistakes could be made, because it is impossible to innovate and simultaneously insist that no mistakes can be made.

This leads me to my second principle, that of risk-taking. My choice for the new Creative Director may be the most obvious example, given that it fell on a person who was unknown and certainly not being considered as a contender for the role. The industry certainly expected the appointment of a renowned talent. I could have played it safe, but as I have always maintained in my career, if I have to be removed from my position, I want it to happen because of a mistake I made, not simply because I took a decision that everyone wanted me to take.

I was looking for someone who would restore Gucci's position as a global fashion authority. In my very first encounter with Alessandro Michele for a coffee and conversation that ended up lasting for over three hours, my instincts told me immediately that he could be the right person.

Thanks to the undivided support of our shareholder, the Kering Group, I took a risk and today can say that that risk has been rewarded, not only from the standpoint of recognition, but also in terms of performance.

Speaking of performance, you can imagine that a company like Gucci generates an enormous quantity of information and indicators. We have all been taught that the more information you have, the more thought-out and far-sighted your decisions can be. However, today there is a danger in thinking that the information we have is never sufficient and that it will not be possible to take decisions without 100% of the information being available.

This approach ultimately leads to a paralysis in decision making that is even worse than making a wrong decision. So, my third guiding principle is to never be afraid to follow one's instincts.

Lastly, and here we come to the theme of this book, I want to address the importance of the product and collections. You can govern all of the numbers and indicators you like, but if there is no sensitivity to the product you will never succeed. This sensitivity must be the basis for building the collection. There cannot be a situation where the Creative Director designs a collection and then at the end of the season the merchandiser says that the best sellers must be made in different sizes or colors.

Dialogue must be constant, in every phase of the process. There must be respect, as I have already said, for everyone's role and contribution, and the organization itself must be considered not as something immovable and fixed, but in constant evolution, a sort of 'learning organization', in which the generation of new ideas and new ways of working is ongoing. This is especially important in fashion, because everything is changing fast, and what works for today does not necessarily work for tomorrow.

The obligation to innovate must be constant, healthy, and present at every level of the organization. When you believe you have arrived and have found the magic formula, you can be sure you are starting to decline.

This is why I recommend the book you are about to read. It concentrates on the product, which is the central aspect of a fashion company. But a product of course reflects the creativity of the designer. And at the same time it is also the expression of the values of the brand and the culture of the company itself – that at Gucci is built upon the values of respect, empowerment, innovation and risk-taking.

Introduction

This book aims to analyze the logics and instruments by which fashion companies create collections, taking into account the variety of companies' characteristics and business models. The collection development process is a critical activity for fashion, that must continuously renew its offering, and is subject to increasingly strict time, cost and quality goals. In addition, this activity impacts all phases of the value chain, from raw materials to distribution of the finished product available to customers, also taking into account the numerous relationships that are established between the operators in the chain. The issue is very relevant at this time, in light of innovations in the scheduling of fashion shows and the timing of introducing new collections onto the market.

The fashion system is a sum of different businesses belonging to different sectors. Indeed, today fashion extends to product areas, such as glasses and cosmetics, that are far from those it represented historically, i.e. textiles, clothing and the part of leather that includes footwear and accessories such as bags, belts and small leather goods. This book concentrates on these historical production chains of fashion, the only deeply linked to a concept of seasons and thus forced to introduce new items each season. In particular, many concepts and examples refer to clothing, where the product is more complex and the production chain is more structured, even though the concepts are easily transferable to footwear and leather goods as well. In addition, even though some international companies are present, many of the examples in the book are drawn from the personal experience developed by the authors in Italy.

Any fashion company must produce at least two collections per year, even though the current trend is towards proposing additional in-season collections, or even to place new articles on sale every one or two weeks. Even when the collection is not completely renewed in each cycle, the rates of presentation and delivery are pressing, leading to considerable management complexity. Other sources of complexity are given by the number of activities that make up the collection development process in its various phases (analysis of sales data, definition of guidelines, collection planning, technical development, and presentation) and the variety of actors involved. The latter belong to almost all company functions. In addition, there are outside actors, such as raw materials suppliers or manufacturers, that can be involved in the development processes. There must also be interaction between the creative and managerial competences present in the company. For all of these reasons, fashion collection development requires uncommon coordination and integration abilities.

The book opens with an analysis of the variety of fashion companies and their processes, to identify best practices and useful recommendations for successful management of collection development. An operational approach is followed, with careful attention paid to the problems that fashion companies must face daily. This book is the product of the work and efforts of various authors, from both the academic and professional worlds. The authors have discussed and shared the contents of the different chapters, seeking to adopt a common language that, without pretending to be universal, can bring some order to the terminological variety of the objects, concepts, tools, techniques and roles relating to fashion. To enrich the text numerous examples have been included, where possible citing the company, or maintaining its anonymity if necessary.

Chapter 1, written by the editors, examines the issue of innovation in fashion, surveying the most recent changes taking place in the sector. Around the perpetual question of stylistic creativity and the organizational philosophies required to sustain it, many new phenomena revolve that generate risks and opportunities for fashion companies, like the compression of development cycles and delivery of collections, the growth of direct distribution, the transformation of events in the sector, attention to sustainability, and also the development of e-commerce and digital activities.

Chapter 2, by Davide Ravasi and Paola Varacca Capello, identifies the most important strategic dimensions that define the variety profiles of fashion companies. In particular, the authors discuss the implications of different logics of interaction with the market, based on the length of lead times and the choice between make to order and make to stock. Organizational options are also presented to effectively define the style-industry relationship and the licensing system. On this basis, the authors outline two approaches to collection development: rational and relational.

Flavio Sciuccati and Paola Varacca Capello are the authors of chapter 3, that is dedicated to the discussion of the activities in the collection development process. This chapter starts with a description of the fundamental elements that define a collection (that is, the positioning and intended target, the style identity, and the collection structure) to then deal with the management problems relating to collection planning, technical development and presentation to the market. Particular attention is paid to the temporal dimension of the process.

Diego Rinallo wrote chapter 4, that looks at the issue of trend formation in the world of fashion. This chapter shows how trends are born through the interaction of numerous actors who mutually influence each other and operate at various levels in the production chain, from fabric producers to trend hunters, from media to distributors, without forgetting celebrities and the consumers themselves. The interaction between these actors is not random, but centered on scheduled events, specific geographic locations and mechanisms of consultation in the sector. There is also an examination of the new role of social media and fashion bloggers.

Chapter 5, by Giorgio Brandazza and Paola Varacca Capello, concentrates on the problem of defining collection guidelines (that should precede the creative development phase) starting with a rational analysis of the sales data. The chapter deals with numerous aspects of sales performance of fashion companies, such as actual price, margins or distribution of sales between models and articles, examining their effects in terms of market positioning and collection complexity.

Chapter 6, by Giorgio Brandazza and Paola Varacca Capello, discusses an essential tool, the merchandising plan, and the figure of the merchandiser. The chapter illustrates the phases of building the plan and the main problems that companies face in preparing it. The plan defines the collection structure and provides indications on the gross margins anticipated, including by defining in detail the relationship between industrial costs, wholesale prices and retail prices. The merchandiser, who at times is given limited organizational power, must therefore perform a delicate connecting role between the initial creation and the development of the collection.

Chapter 7, by Flavio Sciuccati and Paola Varacca Capello, takes an in-depth look at the critical aspects of the collection development process, regarding planning, industrialization and variety. Fashion companies are used to managing pressing schedules and urgent requests, but they increasingly need to shift from informal practices based on personal experience to more formal project management tools. The chapter focuses on techniques for reducing unproductive variety, providing concrete examples and experiences.

We wish to thank everyone who directly or indirectly contributed to the knowledge presented in this book, and in particular the companies Furla (Eraldo Poletto and Rita Paragnani), Moschino (Alessandro Varisco), Fausto Puglisi (Chiara Marangoni), and Tessilform (Emma Ciaponi). We also wish to thank Francesca Bellettini, Filippo Bernasconi, Gianmario Bornei, Pamela Carnelli, Matteo D'Avenia, Enrico Drago, Chiara Mastrangelo, Stefano Miglio, Giona Milani, Veronica Peraro, Massimo Piombini, Paolo Riva, Giulia Salinari, Laura Santanera, Gabriella Saracino, Alessandro Sartori, Mauro Soffià, Ilaria Venturelli and Diana Zanetto: they are the company representatives (we hope we have not forgotten anyone) who have come to the "fashion" halls Bocconi and MAFED over the years, generously sharing their precious experiences with us and the students.

Nicola Misani and Paola Varacca Capello
Bocconi University

1 The Recent Evolution of Fashion

by *Nicola Misani and Paola Varacca Capello*

1. Fashion: products, style and innovation

Fashion refers to all those products characterized by short renewal cycles, divided by seasons, belonging to the sectors of textile-clothing (and its various segments), leather goods and footwear. In these sectors companies renew their product portfolio at least twice a year, alternating between seasons and as a function of specific goals and occasions. The sectors contain segments – such as underwear, pajamas and silk accessories (ties, scarves and foulards) – that follow the seasons less and propose similar products continuously, even though these segments tend to follow fashion more than they did in the past, and tend to accelerate the renewal of the collections.

The sectors are divided into segments by types of products and price ranges: for example, clothing can be divided into *haute couture, prêt-à-porter* (PAP), *diffusion, bridge* and *mass* (Corbellini & Saviolo, 2009). If we look at the highest price segments, we see the overlapping of the worlds of fashion and *luxury*: the most exclusive bags, the most expensive shoes and the dresses modeled in Paris represent luxury in the sectors that are commonly included under fashion.

In principle, luxury products should have quality and style characteristics that are "timeless" (more or less accessible or exclusive in terms of price). However, this does not mean that the luxury segment is not affected by creativity and innovation: *haute couture* shows in particular are the manifestation of creativity free from cost constraints, that through exaggeration strengthen the image of a clothing brand and stress the uniqueness of what it has to offer (Scopelliti, Cillo & Mazursky, 2011).

Given that innovation and creativity are the basis of the phenomenon of fashion, it is necessary to rationally and clearly describe the processes that companies implement to face the challenge of product renewal, combining aesthetic principles with market goals and budget constraints. Current language often confuses the concepts of brand, style, line, product and collection, which we will discuss in detail in the paragraphs and chapters below. The concept of *innovation* must also be properly defined. Innovation varies based on:

- the *activities* involved, and here it is necessary first of all to separate *process* innovation from *product* innovation (Utterback & Abernathy, 1975);
- the *extent* of the change (*incremental* and *radical* innovation, see for example Perrini, 2012);
- the *content* of the change, that allows for distinguishing between *technical, economic, aesthetic* and *symbolic* innovations (Cappetta, Cillo & Ponti, 2006; Verganti, 2009).

Furthermore, innovation may be conceived as a business competence, comparing organizations that prove they are ready to follow new paths with those that, on the other hand, follow, imitate or reinterpret innovations introduced by others (Perrini, 2012).

In recent years fashion companies have been affected by numerous process innovations in supply chain management (principally in order to reduce lead times and working capital), in sales distribution (where the structure of relations between producers and distributors has changed, as have stock turnover policies) and in communication (heavily impacted by digital evolution). Even fast fashion, which we will discuss later, has created innovation in its market approach, with significant repercussions on product development and other internal processes (Tokatli, 2008). After the initial introduction by pioneers and leaders, those process innovations have been adopted over time by all of the competitors, to a greater or lesser extent based on consistency with each entity's reference market and structure.

Other process innovations have regarded design and production systems, such as CAD-CAM systems, automated cutting of fabrics and leather, and digital printing. Despite this, in many cases the assembly phase (i.e. the final production of the clothing item, a pair of shoes or a bag) is still performed by artisans or specialized workers with the assistance of traditional sewing machines or other elementary equipment. Software programs have also been developed, called product life-cycle management (PLM) and product data management (PDM), to provide comprehensive product management, from the design phase through all of the activities and aspects that characterize the process.

Product innovation is what is most relevant for this book, that focuses on the development of the collections of fashion companies. In this context, some innovations have a strictly functional value and regard new types of yarn (as happened with nylon and other artificial and synthetic fibers introduced during the 1900s), new fabrics (that result from new yarns or new weaving and finishing operations) and new non-textile materials (such as Alcantara).

Other innovations, and especially those that follow the rhythms of fashion, regard product *style*. This concept of *style*, that embodies the aesthetic dimension of the product, requires responses to many questions:

- what do we mean by *style*, speaking of collections of clothing items and leather and footwear articles?
- on what elements of the product are stylistic innovation and product development concentrated in fashion companies?
- to what extent do sector trends, rather than designer creativity, influence the process of stylistic renewal of collections by fashion companies?
- if it is true that product renewal is linked to the seasons, is it also true that trends last only one season?
- how do the markets (or segments of demand) chosen by a company as targets, and its brand identity, influence the company's stylistic choices and product development process?

In the language of fashion, style can refer to:

- *dressing* styles;
- what is sometimes called the *look* of the product, i.e. its aesthetic impact.

Dressing styles are linked to historical epochs. Despite there being various labels, we can start by distinguishing between *classic, traditional, modern* (*or contemporary*) and *avant-garde* styles. Classic style is inspired by stylistic precepts defined and linked to the past. Traditional style reinterprets the stylistic precepts of the past, giving them a current expression. Modern style introduces contemporary values in a vision that is still classic, but offers elements of fashion. *Avant-garde* style differs due to its radically new solutions, offered to market segments which are very sensitive to innovation and open to breaking with the past.

With reference to male clothing, the most classic proposals are those that are not as tight on the waist, softer and oriented towards a less youthful target, including in the type of fabrics, that are more traditional. Unstructured jackets, closer fitting lines and more technological fabrics characterize more modern concepts.

In the context of each clothing style, the *look* defines specific styles, which are expressed in elements "of cut (close-fitting, structured, fluid, etc.), color (soft or lively colors), patterns (prints, graphic patterns, flowers, etc.), fabric (synthetic, natural, decorated, rough), and length (referring in particular to skirts and pants: mini, knee-length, ankle-length, etc.)" (Cappetta, Cillo & Ponti, 2003). Style is also defined by accessories: think of the chains of bags, or studs, that have recently become very common.

Some styles recall architectural styles (baroque, *liberty*/art nouveau, etc.), historical periods (empire style), "work" clothes (military style) and so on: a rich vocabulary is developed by the creative designers and the media involved in reading and spreading the fashion. Style understood in this way is interpreted each time according to the dressing styles, the designers' choices and the identity of the brand.

When style means *look*, it offers continuous occasions for innovation, that at times use new functional elements for aesthetic purposes. For example, a light down jacket and leggings were conceived in functional terms to meet needs of comfort and practicality, exploiting technical improvements in materials, but they provided designers the opportunity to offer new aesthetic views.

Stylistic innovations often transmit precise meanings and value messages. The miniskirt, invented at the time of *Swinging London*, embodied an era of female emancipation and protest against rules of behavior considered outdated. Decades earlier, the Poiret *maison* had freed women from the slavery of the corset and the "S-line." On a less epoch-making scale, contemporary stylistic options also frequently have symbolic contents (like the sensuality expressed by Dolce & Gabbana collections).

Each brand (and each designer) has a stylistic identity that each collection interprets based on the new trends proposed. This identity also includes what are called *brand identifiers*, unchanging formal elements that over time become a code for recognizing a brand. This can be a type of product (rubber sole loafers by Tod's, or unstructured jackets by Armani), materials (the *matelassée* in Chanel bags, or woven leather in those of Bottega Veneta), the brand's logo or initials (presented as a pendant, pattern, etc.) or recurring themes (the Eiffel Tower for Louis Vuitton, the magnolia for Chanel, the Medusa for Versace, the Duc carriage for Hermès). A brand's stylistic identity opens up new spaces but also defines the boundaries of innovation, because the designer and his team will always be asked to propose new elements that respect the aesthetic values the brand has acquired over time.

If we want to apply a distinction between radical and incremental innovations in fashion companies, the former are often based on new yarns or materials (think of the role of nylon in the birth of modern women's stockings) or at the level of a single company, new models (of dresses, skirts, pants, etc.) that are completely innovative compared to previous collections. Incremental innovations are those that are limited to modifying existing models or introducing variations in colors, fabrics, patterns or accessories. As we will see, these forms of innovation in fashion entail various types of risk, different abilities to capture trends and clients' needs for new concepts, and above all different degrees of variety and complexity in the process of development of a collection.

2. How fashion is born, and how it evolves

Who creates fashion? What material and symbolic references are used by the creatives who develop products? Does creativity belong to individuals, or is it the result of more complex social mechanisms and dominant styles that more or less consciously shape how new trends are born?

Chapter 4 explains how the entire chain of actors in the fashion world generates trends, defined as macro-trends precisely because they regard the sector as a whole. Those trends are agreed on and proposed each season, and illustrate evolution in society, costumes and lifestyles, translated into specific aesthetic precepts. Not all proposals are valued to the same extent by creatives. Some are ignored, others will be developed by designers and companies, but will fail at the time they hit the market; and still others will be welcomed by the public, becoming popular and long-lasting.

In filtering the proposals accepted in the collections of the various brands, and then launched through communications campaigns, an increasingly important role is played by the media, that includes not only journalists, but also bloggers and celebrities, who speak of new items, wear them or even criticize them, and in any event bring them to the attention of consumers. In turn, consumers play a role of social sharing, participating in defining what is cool at a certain time, undoubtedly influenced by the communication system, but hopefully, also with their own ability to choose and discern.

Research has demonstrated that fashion can go through periods of unrest or uncertainty of aesthetic precepts, and other more stable periods (that can last for a few years) in which a style becomes dominant and establishes itself as a characteristic followed by the majority of creatives (Cappetta, Cillo & Ponti, 2003). For example, between the middle of the nineteen-eighties and the middle of the nineteen-nineties, there was a shift from masculine style, to minimal style, and ultimately to kitsch. This convergence around a dominant style allows the companies and designers who are best at interpreting it to prosper (Cavalli's success in the new millennium is at least in part explained by the popularity of the *animalier* style, a characteristic of this Italian company). To the contrary, those who prove incapable of following the dominant style will find difficulty selling, however much their loyal clients value their creations.

Given the dominant style of a period, the colors, prints, fabrics and other elements of a product also have durations and life cycles. These elements are introduced in a certain season (because they are launched by some producers), and after finding success, are proposed again in subsequent seasons by a growing number of competitors. A topical case is lace, a traditional element relaunched by various brands some seasons ago, that was highly successful and thus stably entered the collections of many companies for multiple seasons. The same reasoning applies to accessories, types and shapes of leather goods, or the height of heels and the roundness of the tips of shoes.

For luxury brands, product innovation is critical but cannot be linked as strictly to trends, to not lose the timelessness associated with this category of goods. The challenge for manufacturers in the luxury sector is to manage this duality between tradition and fashion. The challenge is often resolved by accompanying timeless products, that may have varied very little over the years, with products closer to trends or limited series of ongoing products, where iconic aspects are mixed with new characteristics aimed at a less conservative customer base.

Therefore, if it is correct to say that fashion is a *seasonal* phenomenon, because companies renew collections each season, and the product chain defines the macro-trends at the start of each season, it is just as correct to say that product styles and elements can last longer and define historical periods. This does not mean that stylists do not draw on personal inspiration or their own experiences as well, proposing variety, reinterpretations and also entirely original ideas that can mark the start and the end of certain styles. An interesting example is the "winged" (or trapeze) bag by Céline, created by the designer Phoebe Philo in 2008, and then picked up by all producers in the following years. Figure 1 attempts to summarize the references that feed creativity in fashion products.

Figure 1 The sources of stylistic creativity

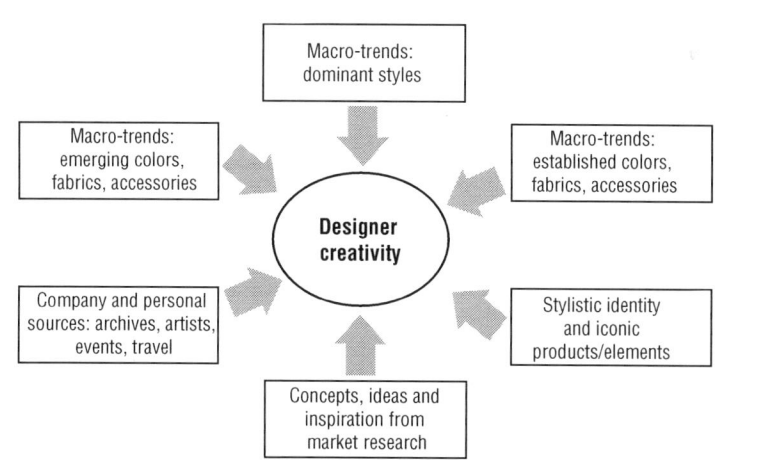

It is also necessary to stress that fashion companies vary based on how they balance creativity and follow styles that become established on the market. This is in part a reflection of the features of the brands, that can have either a more innovative or more commercial identity. To a certain extent it also depends on how the fashion company is internally organized, in particular as regards collection development. A more "artistic" approach can contrast with a more "scientific" approach (Cillo & Verona, 2008), summarized in Figure 2.

In the first approach the creative is dominant, as typically happens in *maisons* founded by a designer. In the second, there is a style office with an extensive team of collaborators and assistants, organized to monitor and interpret new trends. Furthermore, the artistic approach relies on the authority of the creative and his/her individual creations, while the scientific approach is based more on outside stimulus and collective elaboration. The artistic approach, although it can be a source of inefficiency, produces the best results when, thanks to the actual talent of the designer, it is able to define a recognizable and inimitable brand identity. The scientific approach, although it can lead to less original and recognizable products, finds its strength in the ability to follow or anticipate market trends.

Figure 2 Organizational approaches to creativity

	"Artistic" approach	"Scientific" approach
Stimulus to change	Designer	Style office
Locus of research process	Close to the expertise or identity of the designer (e.g. archives)	Distant search: use of trend setters, opinion leaders
Role of individuals	The designer is an "artist"	Collective or repetitive process
Expected results	Develop and consolidate the company's stylistic identity	Changes that anticipate market trends

Source: based on Cillo & Verona (2008).

3. Changes in the system

Fashion also experiences widespread changes both of the concept of fashion products and the methods of their distribution, that transform the dynamics and structures in the sector over the long-term (Merlo, 2003). Probably, the greatest historical innovations of the fashion system were the birth of *haute couture* in Paris at the start of last century, the development of *prêt-à-porter* in Italy in the nineteen-sixties, thanks to a new model of collaboration between companies and designers, and the advent of fast fashion in the last two decades. Fast fashion, which we will discuss below for its implications for collection management, indicates the *modus ope-*

randi of companies able to modify their product assortments at very short intervals. Inditex, that is considered the inventor of fast fashion and is still the leader in this approach, delivers new articles to its stores twice a week, a revolution compared to the old approach of preparing collections twice a year (Ferdows, Lewis, & Machuca, 2004).

Fast fashion has influenced the sector in two ways: greatly shortening product development times and all of the production and logistics processes; and stimulating the consumer to go to stores more often, where he/she is certain to discover something new every time. Fast fashion's ability to offer new items at reasonable prices has fueled the practice of mix & match, in which the consumer pairs costly brand-name articles with fresh, cheap items not likely to last long, but that are in tune with the current fashion and allow for renewing one's look every day.

As a system-wide innovation, fast fashion has accompanied a series of other phenomena in the sector and changes in company strategies. All of the operators, including those less intensely linked to fashion, have been forced to review structure and times of collections, to deal with competition and take advantage of the new opportunities that have arisen.

Apart from the emergence of fast fashion, the current era is characterized by:

- increasingly complex and international competition between companies to win over consumers who are increasingly unpredictable, careful and selective;
- the growing dynamism of manufacturers and the supply chain, demonstrated by the multiplication of fashion weeks and fair events, that have the goal of promoting the offerings of various operators in the supply chain in a targeted way; in fact, a considerable increase is being seen in the number of events, that are increasingly specialized and have more flexible schedules than the traditional appointments (Figure 3); in particular, fashion weeks are no longer only for experts (who had to filter, interpret and transmit them to final customers) but also moments of immediate communication to the public at large;
- the periods of economic crisis that have followed one another in the new millennium in developed economies, and the parallel emergence of Asian consumers as a fundamental market;
- the advent of social networks, mobile devices and e-commerce,

that are transforming communications and the relationship with consumers;
- the development of a new level of sensitivity towards the natural environment and in general towards corporate social responsibility (which we will discuss further in the subsequent section);
- the transformation of the retail system, with the evolution of stores into places for communication, and not only sales, that has led to massive investments by producers in directly operated stores;
- the development of the outlet distribution channel, both as physical stores and through e-commerce.

Figure 3 Increase of sector events

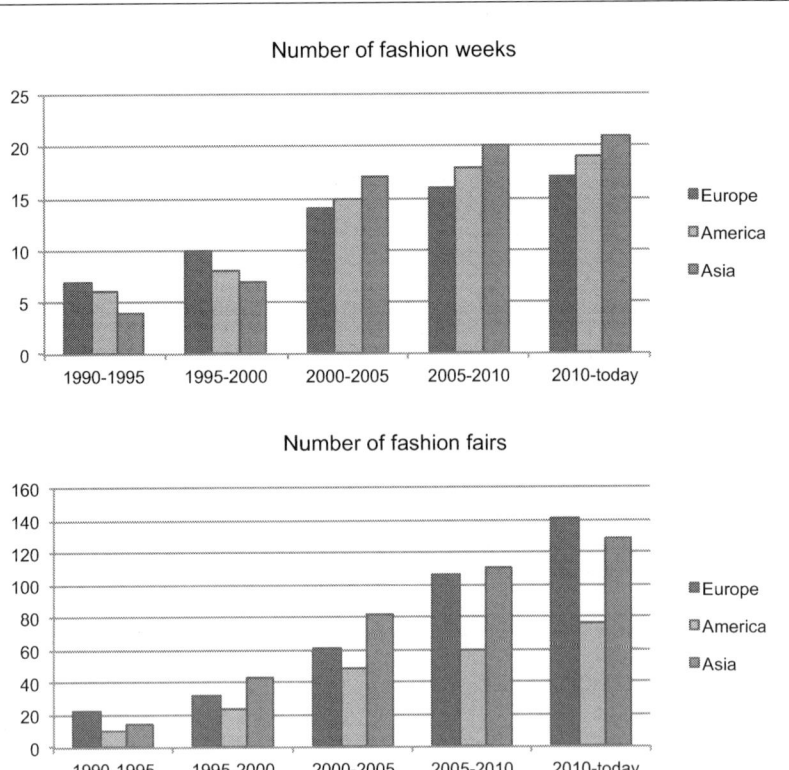

Source: Authors' elaboration of public data.

It should also be observed that, in this complex market context, many traditional and consolidated abilities of fashion companies remain valid and can be exploited and even enhanced. For example, the manufacturing culture of Italian fashion remains an important competitive advantage. After years of searching for low-cost producers in developing countries, we are now seeing a global return to the values of artisanal production. The processing of fabrics, pattern making, embroidery, knitwork and other manufacturing activities reward manual skill and tradition, especially for high-end products. Moreover, a growing desire for product personalization is leading to a revival of tailoring work.

The quality of manufacturing in the Italian fashion system is proven by the foreign companies that choose Italian suppliers, or buy them, or develop production facilities in the Vicenza area, Tuscany, or other districts, stressing the Italian origin of the products in their communication activities. For example, Pierre Denis, the CEO of the English brand Jimmy Choo, has said: "All, and I mean all Jimmy Choo products are produced in Italy, so Italy is the center of our artisanal production. As a luxury brand, focused on accessories, we consider 'Made in Italy' as an essential part of our brand identity and a fundamental sign of the quality of our products" (Misani & Varacca Capello, 2013).

4. Sustainability in fashion

According to Fashion and Luxury Insight (Varacca Capello et al., 2015), the SDA Bocconi and Altagamma report dedicated to fashion and luxury, only 24% of the companies in these sectors publish a sustainability report consistent with GRI (Global Reporting Initiative) standards or other formal reporting standards. The report covers the largest listed international fashion and luxury companies, while excluding family-owned or closed companies where sustainability reporting is even less common. This 24% places the sector well below the average for listed companies, among which approximately 75% of companies in the Global 500 list publish a sustainability report.

The resistance in the fashion and luxury world to meet transparency obligations regarding social and environmental performance, even in large international companies, is surprising if we consider the many critical aspects the sector must face:

- the environmental impact of consumption of materials and energy in textile and leather production;
- the problem of reusing discarded garments;
- the risk that the chemicals used in textile production and tanning can cause harm to human health or fauna;
- the working conditions in the factories and control of the supply chain.

In addition to the transformations already described, the advent of fast fashion has also shortened the useful life of clothing and accessories, leading to an increase in the natural resources used. It is necessary to remember that the production of fibers has a negative impact on the environment. To obtain cotton, the most common fiber, large quantities of water are needed, in addition to pesticides and fertilizers that have negative consequences on the territory and workers. There are also emissions of CO_2 generated in the transport of fibers from countries of origin to those where the subsequent phases of transformation and sale take place, that are often very far away. Some fashion brands have responded to this problem by attempting to use biological cotton, a non-chemical product resulting from less intensive farming practices; however, this only reduces in part the total environmental costs of the fiber.

The most direct way to save natural fibers consists of the cradle-to-cradle approach, by which an attempt is made to give materials new life. The best-known case is that of recycling PET bottles, from which continuous filaments can be obtained for use in clothing (fleece, in particular). We are also seeing renewed interest for natural dyeing techniques, that had fallen into disuse with the spread of synthetic colorants. In addition, some fashion companies are experimenting with biodegradable materials fit for composting. For example, Gucci has introduced biodegradable glasses and shoes, while Puma has announced that it will produce new types of t-shirts and shoes that at the end of their life cycle transform into fertilizers (Carpenter, 2012). For the possibilities of reuse, the most promising technologies are those of artificial fibers, such as polymers, that are derived from fossil fuels but in theory can be recycled infinitely.

These attempts to innovate products to improve their sustainability are in harmony with the gradual emergence of new consumption sensitivities (Rinaldi & Testa, 2013). Nowadays many consumers wish to know how the manufacturer produced a garment, with what materials, in what countries, by whom and in what conditions. New media and social networks drive this need for transparency, because negative information spreads rapidly and acts as a check on business conduct.

The consumer does not want to give up style, emotion, elegance and all of the traditional aesthetic values transmitted by fashion, of course; what the consumer wants, is for these values not to be obtained to the detriment of the environment, and with respect for people. According to some studies, the consumer of sustainable fashion is educated, well-off, has time to dedicate to shopping, and is young but not too young, because he/she must be mature enough to appreciate the cultural meaning of what he/she purchases (Niinimäki, 2010). This opens up opportunities for designers to combine sustainability and creativity, returning materials previously considered poor to the category of beauty and luxury. Stella McCartney is a well-known case of the combination of ethical and aesthetic values, with her broad use of artificial leather in bags and garments with high fashion content (and high price).

At the same time, for the lower ranges of the market, there is an evident conflict between the search for sustainability and the consumer's temptation to purchase fashionable garments at convenient prices. Fast fashion can pull consumers away from thought-out purchases of clothing items, leading them towards "disposable" consumption. A closely related issue is that of working conditions in low-cost countries. The issue became topical after the collapse of the textile factory in Dacca (Bangladesh) in 2013, in which over 1,100 workers lost their lives. The factory produced clothing items for numerous western brands, such as Benetton, Mango, Walmart, El Corte Inglés and Primark (Butler, 2013). The tragedy brought media attention to the structure of the global textile chain, where manufacturing is outsourced to a complex, multi-level network of suppliers, often outside the control of the producer that designs and places its trademark on the product. Exploitation of child labor, suppression of labor union rights, inhuman working hours, insufficient pay, risks to health and dangerous buildings are all possible consequences, despite the fact that many fashion companies have codes of conduct that establish behavior and requirements that suppliers and sub-suppliers must follow.

The origin of the problem is companies' desire to save on costs and increase operating flexibility, through decentralization of production to low-cost suppliers, ready to accept orders with short deadlines. In developing countries these goals translate into pressure on workers. Local governments avoid encouraging social development policies that would increase costs and reduce competitivity of their manufacturers on the global markets. Fashion companies themselves sometimes admit they are not certain that proper working conditions are guaranteed, or that harmful chemicals are not used, given that the factories are located in places where it is impossible to fully monitor their operations.

On the product level, the sustainability profile can represent a source of competitive differentiation, but in the long-term it is destined to become an indispensible characteristic for all producers. The moderate use of sustainability reports among fashion and luxury companies indicates a delay in translating social and environmental problems into organizational solutions, accompanied by goals, performance measurement and control systems. Fashion companies must also abandon a risk management approach (Misani, 1995) in which interventions are only aimed at protecting the brand, and shift to a logic in which sustainability participates in defining the main company processes:

- *product design* (development and industrialization of products with longer duration, with a selection of fibers and fabrics whose processing minimizes environmental impact);
- *branding* (consumer education and involvement);
- *logistics and transport* (inclusion of emissions in efficiency calculations);
- *supply chain* (traceability, transparency, training and monitoring of suppliers of raw materials, components and finished products).

Sustainability rewards above all fashion companies that invest in brand identity and wish to provide consumers with a high-quality experience, that involves not only the product per se, but its intangible qualities, and thus the history of the company and consistency with its heritage (Corbellini & Marafioti, 2013). Countries like Italy, that have a manufacturing culture, can efficiently combine style and sustainability, and capitalize on them to offer stimulus to consumers who are not yet sensitive to these themes but are ready to comprehend excellence. Box 1 presents an initiative by the *Camera della Moda* that goes in this direction.

1 THE RECENT EVOLUTION OF FASHION

Box 1 – The Sustainability Manifesto of the Camera Nazionale della Moda

In 2012, the *Camera Nazionale della Moda* published a Manifesto for the sustainability of Italian fashion. The Manifesto lists and describes ten fundamental principles to ensure the responsible management of fashion products along the value chain.

1. DESIGN. Design quality products that can last a long time and minimize impact on ecosystems.
2. CHOICE OF RAW MATERIALS. Use raw materials, materials and fabrics with high environmental and social value.
3. PROCESSING OF RAW MATERIALS AND PRODUCTION: reduce environmental and social impact of activities and acknowledge everyone's contribution to product value.
4. DISTRIBUTION, MARKETING AND SALE: Include sustainability criteria along the path your product follows to the customer.
5. MANAGEMENT SYSTEMS: Commit to continuous improvement of company performance.
6. FASHION AND NATIONAL ECONOMIC SYSTEM: Support the local territory and Made in Italy production.
7. BUSINESS ETHICS: Integrate universal values in your brand.
8. TRANSPARENCY: Communicate your commitment to sustainability to stakeholders in a transparent way.
9. EDUCATION: Promote ethics and sustainability with consumers and all other interlocutors.
10. Bring the Rules to life

Source: Camera Nazionale della Moda (2012).

5. Impacts on collection development

How are fashion companies reacting to the changes affecting the sector? In particular, what are the impacts of the breadth of assortments, product development collection structure and the respective timeframes? The most common orientation at this time can be summarized as follows:

- a rethinking of the structure of the product offering, especially when divided over multiple lines, to avoid overlapping and reduce costs (the abandonment of the second D&G line by Dolce & Gabbana is a good example);

- a more careful monitoring of the total number of SKUs (stock keeping unit, an approximation of the number of references in the collection, determined by the number of models, fabrics and colors), in order to reduce the complexity of the assortment, and also to make space for an extension of product categories or the introduction of new occasions of use;
- the search for savings in the cost of samples, principally through the reduction of fabric and color variants for the offer presented in showrooms; this policy is favored by new digital solutions that make it possible to also show the client the variants that are not physically available;
- refocusing on iconic products or elements, to strengthen stylistic and brand identity; for high-end companies, this means working more on heritage and less on logo; an example was the relaunching of Burberry in 2006 by the CEO Angela Ahrendts (Ahrendts, 2013), that eliminated licensed products and concentrated on the trench coat, the company's historical strong point;
- the hiring by premium industrial brands of famous creative directors in order to innovate and reinvigorate the stylistic contents of products;
- the review of make or buy choices in collection development activities (design, prototyping, industrialization); as we will discuss below, most companies currently prefer to keep control of the most critical activities or the most complex products, while outsourcing the rest of the phases to qualified suppliers, with long-term relationships, even though approaches differ considerably depending on types of companies;
- review of the structure of seasonal collections, in terms of sales campaigns and delivery times; today most companies propose a pre- and a main season, in addition to a runway (that is generally not sold, to also limit the number of sales campaigns); during the season they produce limited packages (in terms of number of references), called injections, capsules, limited editions, flashes, etc., to continuously renew the assortments and bring the time of purchase by stores closer to the time of sale to final consumers; this trend also leads some companies to make their garments available in the online store immediately after fashion shows (see now, buy now);

- the attempt to combine men's and women's fashion shows, for example at Gucci, with the goal of reducing costs and concentrating in a single event the presentation of products that in any event share the same inspiration.

It follows that product development is no longer necessarily scheduled following classical seasonal timeframes, but can be divided into multiple phases, sometimes using dedicated teams, even in companies that adopt the *programmato* logic. Product development becomes a continuous process of adjustment of the various components of collections, increasingly compressing the time between the conceiving of the product and production and delivery.

Another important trend is producers' investment in networks of directly owned or directly operated stores – known as DOS. The separation between producers, who had their logics and critical activities, and retailers, who had others, essentially no longer exists. The integration between production and retailing, started by fashion retailers, has now been generalized, with two important implications:

- the assortments proposed by fashion companies must be adequate for the needs of DOS, to properly fill the display space and not leave it poorly stocked even at times of more difficult sales;
- fashion companies must learn a new trade, that of the retailer (Brandazza, Rovetta & Varacca Capello, 2010); it is crucial for assortments in the various sales channels to be coordinated and managed rationally in terms of quantities, qualities and times, and delicate choices arise concerning the proper degree of centralization (at company headquarters) or decentralization (in the various local markets) of the assortment choices.

The development of the outlet channel, which allows companies to maintain high mark-ups on new in-season collections and to still use stock in a convenient way, also impacts collections. The companies for which this channel is important have an interest in developing ad hoc products for outlets, to take advantage of the less critical expectations of consumers. This challenge has now become strategic for some brands, especially of leather goods, that propose successful color or material variants of their products in outlets.

The multiplication of international markets also influences collections and management processes. Even though companies desire uniform collections, in order to preserve the brand and style identity, in addition to achieving economies of scale, some markets can require product adjustment. The entry into countries with opposing seasons, large cultural distances, and consumers with very different anthropomorphic characteristics and clothing tastes, can create problems for companies, including with respect to reassortment processes for potential DOS. In addition, despite many emerging countries having significant growth rates, their dimensions do not always initially justify the considerable investments necessary for entry, with the consequence that the company must carefully evaluate times and risks. Mature and traditional markets, where the brand is consolidated, must in any event always be cultivated, including to obtain volumes, turnover and margins that allow companies to invest in emerging countries.

The technological options linked to new devices and applications are constantly evolving and involve above all the processes of communication, sale and collection of information on consumers. Many innovations that are in the experimental phase for now, like virtual mirrors (that make it possible to try on clothes on an avatar), can transform consumers' shopping experience and at the same time enrich knowledge of their tastes, with repercussions on product development. New technologies can also facilitate co-creation, in which consumers are directly involved in the adjustment of products, choosing from a menu of preset options (Fuchs *et al.*, 2013).

Sensitivity towards the environment and corporate social responsibility, in addition to imposing an overall rethinking of production processes and supply chain management, can also translate into new lines for organizing types of products. Examples are offered by "sustainable collections" created by some producers, like the H&M Conscious Collection.

All of these innovations overlap, bringing complexity and dynamism to the sector. However, in a field such as fashion, where aesthetic factors, style and image are of fundamental importance, the specificities of single companies continue to play an essential role in market and financial success.

Bibliography

Ahrendts, A. (2013), "Burberry's CEO on Turning An Aging British Icon into a Global Luxury Brand". *Harvard Business Review*, January-February, pp. 39-42.

Brandazza, G., Rovetta, B., & Varacca Capello, P. (2010), "Moda e lusso: le strategie e i risultati dei più grandi player mondiali". *Economia & Management*, 6, pp. 73-90.

Butler, S. (2013), "Bangladeshi factory deaths spark action among high-street clothing chains", *The Guardian*, 23 June.

Camera Nazionale della Moda (2012), *Manifesto della sostenibilità per la moda italiana*, http://www.cameramoda.it/media/pdf/manifesto_sostenibilita_it.pdf (last access 23 April 2016).

Cappetta, R., Cillo P., & Ponti, A (2006), "Convergent designs in fine fashion: An evolutionary model for stylistic innovation", *Research Policy*, 35, pp. 1273-1290.

Carpenter, S. (2012), "Designers, brands take steps toward sustainable fashion", *Los Angeles Times*, 14 October.

Cillo, P. & Verona, G. (2008), "Search styles in style searching: exploring innovation strategies in fashion firms", *Long Range Planning*, 6, pp. 650-671.

Corbellini, E. & Marafioti, E. (2013), "La CSR nella moda", *Economia & Management*, 3, pp. 62-80.

Corbellini, E. & Saviolo, S. (2009), *Managing Fashion and Luxury Companies*, Etas, Milan.

Dickinson, M.A. & Eckman, M. (2006), "Social Responsibility: The Concept As Defined by Apparel and Textile Scholars". *Clothing & Textiles*, 3, pp. 178-191.

Ferdows, K., Lewis, M.A., & Machuca, J. A. (2004), Rapid-fire fulfillment. *Harvard Business Review*, November, pp. 104-117.

Fuchs, C., Prandelli, E., Schreier, M., & Dahl, D.W. (2013), "All that is users might not be gold: How labeling products as user designed backfires in the context of luxury fashion brands", *Journal of Marketing*, 77(5), pp. 75-91.

Merlo, E. (2003), *Moda italiana. Storia di un'industria dall'Ottocento a oggi*. Marsilio, Venice.

Misani, N. (1995), *Introduzione al risk management*. Egea, Milan.

Misani, N. & Varacca Capello, P. (2013), "Il made in Italy? Chiedetelo agli inglesi", *Via Sarfatti 25*, 11 September, http://www.viasarfatti25.unibocconi. it/notizia.php?idArt=12581 (last access 23 April 2016).

Niinimäki, K. (2010), "Eco-clothing, consumer identity and ideology". *Sustainable Development*, 18, pp. 150-162.

Perrini, F. (2012), *Management. Economia e gestione delle imprese*. Egea, Milan.

Rinaldi, F. & Testa, S. (2013), *L'impresa moda responsabile*. Egea, Milan.

Scopelliti, I., Cillo, P., & Mazursky, D. (2011), "Stupire o persuadere? Strategie di lancio di un nuovo stile nel settore della moda", *Economia & Management*, 5, pp. 67-82.

Tokatli, N. (2008), "Global sourcing: insights from the global clothing industry – the case of Zara, a fast fashion retailer". *Journal of Economic Geography*, 8, pp. 21-38.

Utterback, J.M. & Abernathy, W. J. (1975), "A dynamic model of process and product innovation". *Omega*, 6, pp.639-656.

Varacca Capello, P., Branchini, A., Merlotti, E., & Misani, N. (2015), *Fashion & Luxury Insight*, Sda Bocconi & Altagamma Report, Milan.

Verganti, R. (2009). *Design driven innovation*. Harvard Business School Press, Boston.

2 The Variety of Companies and Collection Development

by *Davide Ravasi and Paola Varacca Capello*

1. Criteria for classifying companies

Fashion companies have very varied characteristics. These characteristics reflect certain variables that influence the way the collection development process occurs. Some variables are linked to the offer that the company presents to the market: the breadth of the product portfolio, the fashion content, the price range, the brand image (also linked to style choices) and its international presence. Other variables reflect structural characteristics of the company and its business management orientation: the company's size, vertical integration, the logic of interaction with the market (*programmato* vs. fast fashion), the distribution logic (retail vs. wholesale), the internationalization of the supply chain, and the relationship between a company's stylistic and industrial attributes. We shall now look at these factors individually.

a) *Breadth of product portfolio*. Many fashion companies propose broad selections in terms of product categories, and develop line and brand extension strategies. A company that originally concentrated on specific products (outerwear, for example), may expand its offering over time to the point of proposing a "total look", with connections that are coordinated and complete with clothing and accessories. In line extension, despite remaining in the apparel sector, for example, collections are increased to meet different needs in terms of price range, function and customer target. In the case of brand extension the brand is extended to various sectors, to include shoes, bags, perfumes, glasses and other products. One example of a portfolio with very broad lines and products is the group led by the designer Giorgio Armani (see Box 1).

Box 1 Giorgio Armani Collections

The apparel offered by Giorgio Armani was divided among six main brands in 2015. Sportswear and children's collections are not considered here.

Brand	Collections
Giorgio Armani Privé	Armani's *haute couture*, that is shown in Paris (one women's collection each season)
Giorgio Armani	The top line, also known as "Black Label," sold only in monobrand stores (one men's collection and one women's collection for each season)
Armani Collezioni	Also called "White Label," this collection has a lower cost than the top line, but is elegant and classic, principally provided to department stores (one men's collection and one women's collection for each season)
Emporio Armani	A young and trendy line, sold in monobrand and multibrand stores (one men's collection and one women's collection for each season)
AJ I Armani Jeans	Denim, sold principally in department stores (one men's collection and one women's collection for each season)
A/X Armani Exchange	The most affordable line, with collections continually renewed based on the fast fashion formula, sold also on the website (men's and women's)

The collections are divided to cover all of the basic product categories (skirts, jackets, shirts, pants, knitted goods, etc.). There are collections produced for specific functions, such as tuxedos (Black Label and White Label). AJ I Armani Jeans and A/X Armani Exchange differ from the rest of the offer because they do not follow the simplicity in design and the preference for soft colors that define Armani's stylistic identity.

Other companies prefer a more limited portfolio, to build and maintain competitive advantages (quality and low costs) in well-defined segments. This choice, especially in small companies, can be advisable in the event of specific characteristics of creative and productive processes in various different categories. For example, womenswear is more complex than menswear, due to its variety of articles and the innovation of models; it follows that there is a need for specific skills that can lead companies to specialize in a single segment.

Even in companies that choose the path of brand extension, it is common for the majority of sales to derive from the original product categories, that remain the core business. These are the categories in which the company continues to directly develop collections. For other business areas it is common to make use of licenses or forms of partnerships in which development is delegated to third parties, generating problems of coordination of styles for related products.

b) *Fashion content*. This variable expresses the stylistic and emotional dimension of the product. Fashion appeals to the search for novelty and trends of the moment. Customers buy fashion articles more for pleasure than for function, knowing that after a short period of time they will not be current anymore. Fashion collections are characterized by continuous stylistic innovation. They require greater effort from companies compared to continuous collections, that are presented each year with little or no variation. Fashion translates into more complex internal organization in companies, in terms of competencies and the number of persons involved (in particular in style, pattern making and prototyping offices), and with greater times and costs for collection development. For continuous collections, on the other hand, intrinsic product quality and efficiency of production are crucial.

c) *Price segment*. High prices allow company style offices more creative freedom, letting them present new looks, new types of workmanship and new materials, even if the product is technically complex and thus expensive to produce. Low prices, or commercial prices, require the adoption of a more rational approach to collection development, in which stylistic creativity is harmonized with the operational needs of materials purchasing and production.

d) *Brand image*. In the world of fashion the brand is particularly important, because it summarizes the stylistic and symbolic dimensions of a product (Tungate, 2008). These dimensions are key variables for customers' decisions to purchase items and pay a higher or lower price for them. The brand image must be consistent with every aspect of a strategy, from product creation to its marketing. In order to maintain the desired image it is not enough for a company to preserve the product's quality and heritage, but the brand must be kept alive with new elements in collections. See the example of Tod's (Box 2).

Box 2 Tod's and brand renewal

> Tod's is an Italian success story in the footwear and fashion sector. The success of the *gommino*, Tod's classic loafer, in the seventies, gave rise to rapid development that led the company to introduce new brands (Hogan's for shoes and Fay for apparel) and to purchase the historic shoe brand Roger Vivier. After 2010 though, growth slowed and margins decreased slightly. According to some observers, the problem was due to a lack of adequate renewal of the Tod's brand.
> In an effort to refresh its image, in 2013 Tod's hired Alessandra Facchinetti (previously with Gucci) to design the women's apparel and accessories collections. The new designer proposed the "D-Cube," an updated version of Tod's classic "D-Bag" (which took its name from Princess Diana). Also in 2013, Tod's appointed a new creative director for men's apparel. The Tod's brand clothing lines are currently offered in only about 15 of the company's over 220 directly operated stores.

e) *International reputation*. International sales allow a company to diversify commercial risk and compensate for low growth rates on the domestic market, as Italian operators discovered after the crisis in 2008. Given the importance of international sales, the company must choose from a global approach, in which to offer the same products on all of the markets, and a differentiated approach, which takes into account specific local tastes, adapting products accordingly (Guercini & Runfola, 2010). In the latter approach, the breadth of the collections must increase. And in any event, delivery times vary in different geographic markets due to differences in climate and distributors' policies, leading to complexity in the collection development process.

f) *Company size*. This variable is important in all industrial sectors, because it determines the extent of resources that can be spent for investment. In fashion, size constraints affect the potential breadth of collections, for example, since the number of references (or SKUs) determines the financial needs linked to working capital and customer service.

g) *Vertical integration*. Fashion companies must monitor four fundamental activities: product development, manufacturing, distribution and brand management. The activities may be directly or indirectly controlled, through contracts or partnership with outside companies. Many fashion companies developed around one of these activities and then decided to invest in the direct control of additional activities. Consider the numerous *maisons* (such as Armani, Dolce & Gabbana or Versace) that began with creative product development and gradually integrated until they directly controlled production (for at least part of the collections) and established their own stores. This allowed them to enrich product development and go in new directions. An example is having their own stores, that allows for rapidly collecting information on demand, that otherwise would not be directly available, and developing a sensitivity for the market that eludes those who use indirect channels. At the same time, there is the problem of preparing collections that, in terms of breadth and delivery times, are suitable for distribution without intermediaries.

Fashion companies have ample possibilities to outsource any type of activity to suppliers, including product development. Some companies limit themselves to formulating creative input, managing merchandising (that initially coincides with the definition of selections) and controlling the final result, delegating to third parties research on fabrics, pattern making, prototypes and industrialization. The third party generally also manages production.

h) *The logic of interaction with the market*. There is a contrast between the logic of *programmato* collections and fast fashion. In the former, the company creates the collection, presents it to distributors and begins production only after having collected orders from them. The process takes place before the sales season. In the latter, the collection is created and produced during the sales season, rapidly responding to the emerging trends on the market, and sold to end-users in its own or affiliated stores, or to independent distributors, including through specialized wholesalers. This variable will be discussed further in section 2.

i) *Distribution logic*. There is a contrast between retail and wholesale orientations (Rath, Petrizzi, & Gill, 2012). The former characterizes those companies that conduct the majority of their sales through directly operated stores (DOS) and online stores, while the latter regards companies that work primarily through independent multibrand stores or franchisees. The pure case of retail orientation is that of numerous fashion retailers, such as Zara, H&M and Uniqlo, that only use DOS (with the exception of small percentages of franchising in some countries). We have briefly mentioned some of the advantages and disadvantages of directy operated stores regarding vertical integration. We must add that companies with a retail orientation develop a particular sensitivity for the needs of stores, that become the starting point for all operating processes, including collection development. In addition, the more distribution is carried out through direct channels, the more limited the activity of presenting collections and gathering orders will be.

j) *Internationalization of the supply chain.* In recent decades fashion has developed a complex and decentralized supply chain, in which low value-added production is located in countries with low labor costs. Decentralization abroad is easier when a *programmato* logic is adopted, because production takes place well in advance of sales, and the long times required for shipping from countries like Bangladesh or China are acceptable. In the area of *programmato* collections, the permanent nature of the activity allows for more offshoring of high-fashion content models, because large volumes can be produced with the accumulation of stock. As shown in Figure 1, many Italian companies still maintain most of their production in our country, either due to the high fashion content of their products, or the need for high-quality manufacturing. In recent years we have also seen a partial return of production to Italy (reshoring), especially for higher value-added products and activities.

k) *The style-industry relationship.* This relationship involves various different arrangements, from *maisons* that are vertically integrated to industrial and commercial brands that make use of different creative options, to companies that produce on license and thus lack internal sources of creativity. Section 3 is dedicated to this complex issue.

2. The logic of interaction with the market

The distinction between *programmato* and fast fashion is one of the best-known concepts in the fashion sector. Some clarifications will be useful, however. In every industrial sector some companies operate with a 'make to order' (or 'pull') logic, and others with a 'make to stock' (or 'push') logic. The former wait for client orders before producing, while the latter produce in advance, assuming stock risk. If we consider the concepts of:

- lead time (the time between order acquisition and delivery)
- time to market (the time between the conceiving of the collection and delivery)

Figure 1 Supply chain of the largest Italian fashion companies

	% of production in Italy	Foreign countries used for production
Aeffe	100% (excluding finishing); Pollini (shoes) 80%	China, Eastern Europe
Armani	Giorgio Armani: 100%; Armani Collezioni and Emporio Armani: 70%	China, Romania, Peru, Thailand, Tunisia
Benetton	10%	China, Croatia, India, Tunisia, Turkey
Brioni	100%	
Burani	Apparel 90%; footwear 90%; bags 85%	Far East, Eastern Europe
Canali	100%	
Corneliani	100%	
Dolce & Gabbana	Dolce & Gabbana: 100%; shoes and bags: 78%; D&G: apparel 20%, footwear and bags: 70%	Far East, Eastern Europe, Mediterranean countries
Ferragamo	100%	
Gucci	95%	n.a.
Miroglio	Apparel 20%	n.a.
Prada	71%	Far East, Eastern Europe, Mediterranean countries
Valentino Fashion Group	Valentino: 100%; Red: 65; MCS: 10-20%	Eastern Europe
Zegna	Zegna: 70%; Agnona: 100%	Asia, Mexico, Romania, Spain, Switzerland, Turkey

Source: Sacchi (2010).

we can state that *programmato*, the traditional logic in the sector, has long lead times (3-4 months) and even longer times to market (9 months). In fast fashion, lead times are greatly reduced (2-6 weeks), since production takes place before order acquisition; time to market is shortened if the collection is successful, but the company exposes itself to the risk of unsold goods if the product fails to properly interpret trends and is not favorably received by clients. Fast fashion began to take hold in Italy in the nineties, in the lowest price segment on the market, through producers who presented themselves as intermediaries for stores, offering them the possibility to supplement their collections during the season. Fast fashion is thus a different model than the one adopted by large international fashion retailers, because it was born to serve retailers, not final customers.

If we compare the concepts of lead time and make to order vs. make to stock, we can construct the following grid, that enriches the distinction between *programmato* and fast fashion and shows the emergence of two other models applied concretely in various companies.

Figure 2   Models of interaction with the market

	Make to order	Make to stock
Long lead time	Programmato	Fast delivery
Short lead time	Reassortment	Fast fashion

The overall picture is thus the following.

- *Programmato*: this is the typical mode especially of prestigious *maisons* and brands; it involves long times. The presentation of collections takes place in January and February for fall/winter (FW) and between July and September for spring/summer (SS). Order collection, production and delivery occur between February and September for FW, and between September and January and March for SS (the timing of deliveries also depends on the specific features of the various markets). The advantages are that production is based on orders, production times are long, and cash flow is predictable; the main disadvantage is that the company does not seize upon the latest market trends.
- *Fast delivery*: the company decides to take a risk on certain articles, producing them before having sales results in stores (sell-in). The lead time is traditional, while time to market is reduced, allowing the company to more freely schedule production and satisfy part of seasonal sales with stock. Fast delivery lends itself to articles where the risk of unsold goods is low, such as continuous items supported by large advertising campaigns.
- *Fast fashion*: fast fashion manufacturers sell in season, do not produce based on orders, and have very short lead times. This offers

the following benefits: less complexity in product development, especially where there is no research and the style office limits itself to copying the successful seasonal articles of other brands; the product is always up-to-date; and the financial cycle is shorter. There are some critical aspects: it is necessary to develop excellent relations with fabric suppliers, so that they will be ready to satisfy even unpredictable orders of materials on short notice; production needs to be rapid, which assumes direct control of the same (like in Zara) or a coordinated network of *Façonistas* (laboratories or small companies specialized in one or more phases, such as cutting, sewing, embroideries, dyeing, etc.).

- *Reassortment*: this entails rapid delivery of the articles in the collection, based on orders from the retailer. It allows for spreading production over a longer period of time, with advantages in terms of use of production capacity and reduction of stock and financial needs. It assumes advanced approaches to production that allow for a rapid response to client orders. For example, some manufacturers share stock information with suppliers, who then act based on products delivered downstream.

An additional type is *Pronto programmato*, a mixed method in which fast fashion is produced with some *programmato* collections, to avoid the limits of the fast model. An historic example of this approach is Patrizia Pepe (see Box 3a).

Box 3a. Patrizia Pepe and the birth of *pronto programmato*

Tessilform was born in 1990 as a producer and distributor of clothing items. In 1993 the company created the Patrizia Pepe brand, dedicated to fast fashion. Sales to retailers were initially conducted through the company's own showrooms in Bologna, Florence and Milan. The offer concentrated only on womenswear, and on jeans in particular. The only sizes available were 40, 42 and 44. The company made up for this limit by rapidly renewing the collections, with 15-20 new models produced every week.
Thanks to the products' success and the development of a strong brand identity, the company decided to introduce traditional collections, to be presented and sold before the start of the season. At the same time, the aim was to maintain strength in the fast fashion segment. The timeframe for the collections took the form shown in the figure below. In each season (the figure refers to SS), Pepe presented: a) a

main collection, sold with a timeframe similar to that of *programmato*; b) a 'flash' collection, sold in late fall and delivered in March; c) approximately twenty weekly mini-collections with a fast fashion logic, sold and delivered to stores during the season, until the end of May or the beginning of June. Note that in fashion jargon 'flash' collections are small collections created and sold during the season to supplement the main collections.

Patrizia Pepe SS collections

	June	July	Aug	Sept	Oct	Nov	Dec	Jan	Feb	Mar	Apr	May
Main collection		▓	▓	▓					▓	▓		
		order							delivery			
Flash collection						▓			▓	▓		
						order			delivery			
Weekly mini-collections												
								immediate availability				

SS Collection based on *programmato* logic

	June	July	Aug	Sept	Oct	Nov	Dec	Jan	Feb	Mar	Apr	May
Collection		▓	▓	▓					▓	▓		
		order							delivery			

Source: Corbellini (2006).

Today Patrizia Pepe, following continuous expansion on foreign markets, has in part modified its offer structure, giving more room to the main collections and reducing the number of intra-seasonal collections (Box 3b).

Box 3b. The evolution of Patrizia Pepe

After having operated almost exclusively in women's fashion for the first ten years, Patrizia Pepe subsequently expanded its collections. Menswear dates from SS 2005, children's clothing from SS 2007, and women's underwear from FW 2008-2009. 2011 saw the debut of the perfume line, while in 2012 the new brand Loiza was launched, but the marketing of the brand was recently interrupted. The group's core business remains women's apparel. In the last ten years the group has undertaken a strong process of expansion and now has four showrooms in Italy (Milan, Florence, Asti and Padua) and six foreign branches between Europe (Belgium, France, Germany and Switzerland), Russia and Asia (China and Hong Kong) with six other diffusions, responsible for their own reference markets. The group has more than 400 employees and is managed completely by the family. At the end of 2015 turnover was 118 million euro, with pre-tax income of 12 million euro. Even though Patrizia Pepe was born as a fast fashion company, with the characteristic of continuous renewal of collections (15-20 new models every week), over time its success allowed it to introduce traditional collections, to be presented and sold at the start of each season. In recent years the internal market has undergone a revolution, driven by changes in consumption. Final customers seem to show less interest for last-minute new items and tend to leave purchases until the end of the season, in part due to the economic crisis. Retailers have significantly reduced reassortment during seasons, to avoid the risk of unsold stock. That trend has led to a strong reduction, and almost the disappearance, of fast fashion, in favor of *programmato* collections. The Patrizia Pepe brand, whose success is linked to fast fashion, has felt the effects of this evolution and now survives almost exclusively on *programmato*. The offer concentrates on two types of *programmato* collections named Preview and Main, characterized by a different time lag with respect to the start of the traditional sales campaigns period, of approximately nine and six months. Recently a Fast collection was also reintroduced to reassort stores with new products.

The company directly manages all of the phases of research, style and prototyping. Physical production is conducted outside of the company by a pool of selected suppliers. Geographically, while the suppliers of the residual fast fashion collections are generally in the Prato district in Tuscany, a significant portion of the *programmato* collections (approximately half of the total) are produced by suppliers in countries with low production costs, both in Europe and Asia.

The order and delivery timeframes for the collections are as follows:

FW 2016 – Sales campaign

– Preview: end of October 2015 – start of December 2015
– Main: end of January 2016 – mid-March 2016
– Accessories: end of January 2016 – mid-March 2016
– Men's: mid-January 2016 – mid-March 2016

FW 2016 – Delivery of goods to store

– May 2016 – end of September/October 2016

SS 2017 – Sales campaign

– Preview: start of May 2016 – end of June 2016
– Main: start of July 2016 – end of September 2016
– Accessories: start of July 2016 – end of September 2016
– Men's: mid-June 2016 – mid-September 2016

SS 2017 – Delivery of goods to stores

– December 2016 – March/April 2016

The distribution system is organized on a geographical basis so that each subsidiary is responsible for its own markets. From the beginning, the wholesale distribution

> made use of "diffusions", spaces in which samples of the collections are displayed and pre- and post-sales service is provided to clients. Since the FW 2012 season, distribution at the wholesale level in European markets has undergone a profound change. Before then diffusions were actual wholesale centers, that purchased the products from the group leader and then resold them to their clients. Subsequently, Italian and European diffusions were transformed into sales agents: Tessilform Spa sells directly to final clients and diffusions perform the function of agents and are compensated with a commission.
> The company also makes use of a retail sales network divided into its own stores (managed by the group leader and the subsidiaries) and monobrand stores managed by independent operators through franchising agreements. The network includes various flagship stores in the prestigious locations of international fashion. There are 14 stores managed by Tessilform, there are 38 managed in Europe, Russia and Asia by subsidiaries, and there are 60 stores managed through franchising or affiliations spread around the world. There are also 13 outlets between Italy and the rest of the world.

Source: compiled by Emma Ciaponi, based on information from the company.

3. The style-industry relationship

In sectors where competition plays out on the aesthetic and expressive attributes of a product, success requires a delicate integration between creativity, managerial skills and entrepreneurship (Varacca Capello & Ravasi, 2002). Yet creativity demands freedom to experiment and is difficult to channel into a system of rules, procedures and deadlines. The managerial approach to a company requires organization, method and predictability, and often clashes with the unwillingness of creative individuals to submit to the company's time schedule. Entrepreneurship, in addition, requires attention and sensitivity to the market and its needs; concentrating too much on the market - on different tastes or trends underway - can however reduce creative ability and make it hard to propose truly innovative styles and concepts. On the other hand, the development of balanced company structures and successful collections depends precisely on the composition of the contrasts between these three essential skills.

The analysis of the relationship between creativity, managerial skills and entrepreneurship can be conducted on two levels. First of all, we can consider the different options available to the main contributors of creative skills (the designers) to integrate their work with those who are able to bring their designs to life, i.e. the manufacturing companies, that contribute managerial, productive and sales abilities. Secondly, we must consider the collection development process, where these abilities come together operationally in the creation of the product.

Despite the variety of the agreements and contractual forms that bind the various actors, it is possible to identify some company models through which operators in the sector attempt to simultaneously cover the stylistic, managerial and entrepreneurial dimensions. The most significant models, including in terms of economic dimensions, seem to be:

- integrated *maisons*, that are led by the designers and directly manage development of the product, and also production and distribution, at least in part;
- industrial or commercial brands, in which creative activity is carried out both by teams of internal designers and by freelance designers;
- licensing relationships, in which the designer makes use of the structures of a manufacturing company not only for production or distribution, but also for the development of his/her own collections;
- forms of art directorship, in which an industrial enterprise or a *maison* entrust the direction and coordination of all of the activities aimed at defining and developing its brand identity to a designer, often a well-known, prestigious name.

From the designer's point of view, various options exist to put his/her creative gifts to use (see Figure 3). Many designers begin their careers as in-house designers, that is, as employees of the style office of a manufacturing company or *maison*; this solution offers a guarantee of continuity and dedication to the structure to which the designer belongs.

There are also many designers, both well-known and not, who work as freelancers, offering their creative consulting to a large or small range of companies, that in this way solve the problem of renewal of their collections. A freelance designer provides inspiration and fashion tendencies to an internal product office, that carries out the other research and development activities. The relationship may be continuous, or not. This situation is widespread also in many other sectors where design plays a significant role: an industrial designer rarely concentrates on only one type of prod-

Figure 3 Organizational options for the designer-company relationship

Organizational options for designers
Maison (well-known designers)
Art directorship (well-known designers)
Company design team (as member of a team): young or emerging designers
Freelancers: young or emerging designers

Organizational options for companies (industrial and commercial)
Licensees (for the *maisons*)
Hire art director to design company collections
Build an internal design office
Use freelancers
Mix of all solutions

Source: Varacca Capello, Guerini, Misani, & Ravasi (2013).

uct, having relationships with multiple companies, including well-known ones, in which the product is distinguished by the double recognition of the signatures of the producer and the designer.

In all of these cases the designer provides his/her skills to consolidated organizations, without assuming responsibility for the development, production and distribution of the collection.

If, on the other hand, the designer becomes sufficiently famous to sign and market his/her own collection, we speak of a *maison*. The designer then has the problem of accessing the production capacity and structures that manage the activities of communication, sales and distribution. The least demanding solution consists of licensing one's *griffe* to a manufacturing company, that supports the development of the collection and takes care of the production and sales activities. The designer maintains control of the creative activities, often supported by a team of associates. The *maison* also manages and promotes the brand image.

Young emerging designers often rely on licensees, primarily because their initial sales would not be able to cover the fixed costs linked to product development and production. Furthermore, through a licensing contract they have access to a range of industrial and commercial abilities that allow them to grow and help them make a name for their *griffe*. Even successful *maisons* such as Moschino and Valentino have continued to use this method for a long time, before becoming integrated industrial organizations. Others, like Roberto Cavalli, continue to use licensees (see Figure 4).

Even *maisons* that end up directly managing the industrial production of their own collections use licenses for the development and production of goods outside of their core business and original know-how (glasses, perfume, cosmetics). The establishment of a licensing relationship however requires careful management of the contract by the licensor, both in strategic terms and through definition of the areas to which one's brand is to be extended, and in operational terms, as regards control of the activities carried out by the licensee (Colucci, Montaguti, & Lago, 2008).

The alternative to licensing is direct control (that can be implemented in various forms) of the companies that manage production and sales activities, through the creation of a fully integrated *maison* that controls all phases, from product development to sales. Armani, Dolce & Gabbana, Prada and Versace are examples of designers who have preferred this development model, although with different timeframes and methods.

However, the construction of an integrated *maison* forces the designer to deal with the problem of the acquisition of managerial and entrepreneurial competencies, and the delicate management of relationships with business organizations. Indeed very few designers seem to bring creative, entrepreneurial and management skills all together: Giorgio Armani may be the only successful example. His initial experience at La Rinascente and Cerruti allowed him to develop a significant wealth of technical and business knowledge, that he was then able to combine with an uncommon fashion sensitivity. Other talented designers have exploited the complementary skills of their family members, or personal partners, thus keeping complete control of business and creative aspects in-house, so to say. For example, the entrepreneurial talents of Santo Versace, Gianni's brother, or of Patrizio Bertelli, Miuccia Prada's husband, have played an essential role in the development of the two companies. When he began his activity, Armani himself found important support from his partner and companion Sergio Galeotti.

It should be noted that many integrated *maisons* use licensees for the development and production of items that require particular technical skills (for example shoulder garments and shirts) or for minor collections (underwear, beachwear, etc.). Furthermore, in most cases the management of creativity is essentially carried out by a team of designers in which, along with the owner of the *maison*, various collaborators with different specializations work on broad collection projects.

Figure 4 The evolution of licenses in some Italian fashion companies

The following tables describe the evolution of the licenses of some historic Italian companies in certain business sectors. The first refers to 1998, the second to 2012. The comparison shows that some companies, such as Armani and Dolce & Gabbana, have gradually given up licensing, in favor of vertical integration. Others have extended the use of this practice in pursuing growth through line and brand extension (Cavalli, Trussardi, Versace).

1998

	Women's	Men's	Children's	Underwear	Beachwear	Shoes	Leather goods	Other accessories	Eyewear	Perfume and cosmetics
Dolce & Gabbana, D&G	Dolce Saverio; Ittierre	Dolce Saverio; Ittierre		Le Bonitas	Le Bonitas	Sergio Rossi + other licensee n.a.	Fontana + other licensee n.a.	Isa Seta; Itierre	Marcolin	Euroitalia
Trussardi		Corneliani				Baldinini		Mantero	Visibilia	
Giorgio Armani, Collezioni, Emporio Armani	Vestimenta; GFT	Vestimenta; GFT	Licensee n.a.	Licensee n.a.	Licensee n.a.	Licensee n.a.	Licensee n.a.		Luxottica	L'Oréal
Versace, Versus, VJC	Ittierre	Ittierre				Itierre + other licensees n.a.	Itierre + other licensees n.a.		IC Optics	
Roberto Cavalli, Class, Just Cavalli	Dressing; Ittierre	Dressing; Ittierre + other licensees n.a.								

2012

	Women's	Men's	Children's	Underwear	Beachwear	Shoes	Leather goods	Other accessories	Eyewear	Perfume and cosmetics
Dolce & Gabbana, D&G									Luxottica	P&G Prestige
Trussardi		Vestimenta	Idea			Le Mazza Mirella		Mantero	Charmant	ICR - ITF
Giorgio Armani, Collezioni, Jeans, Junior, Emporio	JV with Vestimenta	JV with Vestimenta and Zegna		Wolford					Safilo	L'Oréal
Versace, Versus	Facchini	Zegna; Facchini		Le Bonitas	Le Bonitas	Facchini	Facchini	Facchini	Luxottica	Euroitalia
Roberto Cavalli, Class, Just Cavalli	Dressing; Staff International	Gibò; Dressing; Staff International	Simonetta	Isa Seta; Albisetti	Isa Seta; Albisetti	Calzat. Elisabeth; Rodolfo Zengarini; Staff International	Compagnia delle pelli; Staff International + other licensee n.a.	Isa Seta; Albisetti	Marcolin	Coty Prestige

Source: elaboration using information from the press and company websites.

Many *maisons* that do not pursue the path of integration are at a certain point acquired by industrial groups, as has happened in the past with Ferrè, Romeo Gigli and Valentino, to mention just a few. Sometimes the buyer is the same as the licensee. For example, in 2000 Gianfranco Ferrè was acquired by GTP (Gruppo Tonino Perna) and in 2002 it was integrated into IT Holding. More recently, Marni was bought by Only the Brave, Renzo Rosso's group, that includes Diesel and Staff International, that carries out licensed production for various Italian and foreign brands.

Another fundamental problem that a *maison* must deal with sooner or later is succession, after the founder is no longer present. In Italy, Moschino was the first to have to face this problem, only 11 years after the birth of the company. Despite not having followed the path of integration, Moschino had a team that worked well together for the development of collections and for communication. The members of the team guaranteed brand continuity, under the leadership of Rossella Jardini, who had worked with Franco Moschino from the beginning. An alternative solution is represented by the involvement of outside designers as art directors, as happened at Valentino for example, after the founder departed (see Box 4). In this case, it is important for the new designer to faithfully follow the brand memory, drawing from the company's historical archives, but at the same time injecting new thinking and originality in his/her creations.

Some successful designers, having already built up a professional history and a solid reputation, are called on to manage product development and coordinate marketing and communication activities for a fashion company. This is common for industrial brands, that do not have an original creative identity. In *maisons*, this happens not only to replace a deceased or departing founder, but also to support and renew historic labels, like Chanel or Yves Saint Laurent. For these companies turnover comes from perfumes, cosmetics or accessories, more than from apparel. Collections however remain important for communication, because the design and elegance of the clothing articles reinforce the brand's values and redefine its attributes from a modern standpoint. This model, that is typical of historic French companies, has been successfully reproposed at Gucci, thanks to the precious work of Tom Ford.

Although in many of these cases the figure of the art director was instituted only after the exit of the founder, the creation of this position can also be used by designers who wish to create a future for their name

Box 4. The stylistic succession to Valentino

Valentino Garavani and his partner Giancarlo Giammetti withdrew from the Valentino Fashion Group company in 2007, shortly after being acquired by Permira, a well-known English private equity fund. Both of the founders disagreed with the line that Permira wanted to adopt for the development of the company. The new creative director was chosen without the consent of Garavani, who had created the company and manned the creative helm for over forty years.
The next two years were difficult: sales declined and the company went into the red. Permira was forced to write down the original value of the acquisition by more than 50%. At the end of 2008 two new creative directors were named: Maria Grazia Chiuri and Pierpaolo Piccioli. Both had grown up in Fendi, had entered the Valentino Fashion Group in 1999, and had worked alongside Garavani for eight years with responsibility for accessories. Starting with their first collections, the stylistic line chosen by the new creative directors openly reconnected with the brand's stylistic heritage.
Under this stylistic direction and thanks to the entry of new shareholders in 2012 (Mayhoola, a fund controlled by the ruling family of Qatar), the company returned to growth and restored financial balance. A sales development plan is currently underway for the opening of new flagship stores in the most important fashion capitals.

Source: Filippetti (2015), abridged from.

for when they will no longer directly manage new projects. It is not easy though, to identify a person who can play this role, that is, to interpret a style without betraying it, especially when the designer who created the *maison* is still present.

The different forms of organization presented are different ways of combining creativity, entrepreneurial qualities and managerial skills. Considering the spread of the various models, none of them seem to be clearly superior to the others: the efficacy of each model depends on a company's characteristics, its leading actors, its products and the profile of the designer (see Figure 5). On a strictly financial level, the forms that allow for keeping creative and entrepreneurial factors together, offer the advantage of controlling industrial margins; through licensing contracts the creative designer receives royalties (which must cover a series of investments in communication and image, though), even though the licensee must be very efficient with management, lest margins fall, which are already burdened by the royalties.

Figure 5 Advantages and disadvantages of the various forms of organization

Forms of organization	Advantages	Limits
Integrated maisons	• Control of supply chain • Proximity to market (when distribution is controlled) • Appropriation of value generated by manufacturing activities	• Difficulty of managing entrepreneurship and management of the group • Management of succession • Need for considerable financial resources • Rigidity of structure
Industrial brands		
– with internal style offices	• Easy to coordinate between company functions • Direct control of development process • In tune with the company and its brands	• "Limited" innovation • Poor contact with the market (if distribution is not controlled) • Difficult to achieve stylistic leadership
– with freelance designers	• Unconstrained innovation • Multiple sources of innovation • Flexible structure	• Poor coordination with other company functions • Difficult to control development • Stylistic continuity at risk
Licensing relationships		
– for the licensor	• Access to technical and sales skills • Limited investments and flexibility of structures	• Licensee does not meet the brand's needs • Different goals
– for the licensee	• Opportunity for expansion to new market segments • Opportunity to exploit skills and production abilities • Access to stylistic skills	• Difficult management of "creative" personnel • Need to build a balanced portfolio of licenses and/or own trademarks to reduce risks deriving from the loss of a license
Forms of art directorship	• Opportunity for managerial development of a brand/label lacking the figure of designer • Relaunch of a brand • Method of managing succession in a maison	• Difficult to identify a person able to perform the role in harmony with the brand/label

Source: Varacca Capello & Ravasi (2002).

4. Organizational roles

While the combination of creative, entrepreneurial and managerial competencies we have discussed is achieved primarily through the adoption of a specific configuration of the command structures, effective integration of creative, managerial and entrepreneurial factors depends on the method by which companies concretely manage the balance between creativity and industrialization needs in the collection development process (Saviolo & Testa, 2000). Various skills contribute to this process: some are specialist skills, linked to the product and the relationship with the market; others involve coordination, linked to internal organization, planning and control of activities (Granger, 2012). Figure 6 summarizes the main competencies and their respective roles.

Figure 6 Competencies and roles in the collection development process

Competencies	Roles
Stylistic/creative/ideational	Designer, style office
Sales/marketing	Brand manager, sales director, merchandiser
Production methods/industrialization	Pattern making, prototyping, technical offices
Production processes (internal and external)	Production directors
Procurement/purchases	Style office (samples, collection), purchasing office (supplier management)
Coordination	Product manager (uomo/donna prodotto), fashion coordinator
Planning and valuation	Planning director, management control

Each company attributes specific contents to the single roles, and there are various organizational solutions for the structure of the offices. The adoption of one or another model entails differences in terms of roles, in the sense that some figures may appear or have different skills in some solutions rather than in others. In chapter 6, we will examine in particular the figure of the merchandiser, which has become critical and very sought-after in the past decade. Furthermore, responsibilities can be divided by product categories or by type of collection (for example using dedicated teams for pre-collections and main collections).

If we return to the previous classification of organizational models, an integrated *maison* generally follows a layout similar to that of the art directorship, in which the designer has high seniority and a hierarchical position. This figure coordinates and supervises the operations of a creative team that follows the guidelines he/she has set out.

In licenses, on the other hand, the roles that interface between the designer, his/her staff and the licensee company, are necessary and important. In *maisons* of a certain size, there is generally a person responsible for licenses, who coordinates the directors focused on single products. In licensee companies, specialists coordinate and operationally manage the single collections; if the collections are very complex or there is more than one for a single brand, there can also be a brand manager to supervise the relationship (Giannelli & Saviolo, 2001).

In industrial companies with their own brands, coordination of the collection development activities is facilitated also by the physical proximity of the persons who have the different competencies; and even in the case of involvement of external designers, the company's style office manages this contribution in a structured manner, from a dominant position.

The type of product - the number of collections, the market segment, the type of collection (formal womenswear, menswear, and so on), etc. – also has a significant influence in determining the most suitable organizational solution to carry out the development activities. Licensees that have multiple active licenses are often organized with dedicated structures (style office, search for fabrics and accessories and then selection of suppliers, pattern making, sales offices) for each license, so as to guarantee maximum focus for each designer. Other companies, that manage multiple brands, including their own and licensed brands, can opt for solutions in which a part of the structure is shared, when the type of product allows. This is what happens at a company that manages different brands, for example, which are all centered on a casual-type product though. As regards pattern making and industrialization, the development process is managed in offices divided by type of garment: shirts, pants, jackets, etc. The more creative activity, that defines trends, comes up with shapes and colors, is managed separately for each brand, so as to guarantee efficiency of development, but also consistency and strength from the brand standpoint.

5. The rational or relational approach to collection development

The development process can be managed with two different approaches (Varacca Capello & Ravasi, 2002). Certain companies have formal tools for coordination, they conduct detailed market analysis, and carefully schedule the various activities. Others follow a more personal approach, where the experience of the people involved and their ability to manage complex situations play a key role, relying on the active participation of those individuals.

We can define the first approach as "rational", and the second as "relational", precisely to highlight the substantial difference in the structures and procedures adopted. The first is based on detailed planning of activities, careful cost control and the systematic exploitation of synergies between the different functions at the division level. The second is characterized by greater independence of each unit and by the decisive role played by the know-how, experience, motivation and relational skills of the people involved. Figure 7 provides a schematic view of the structures, processes and tools that are typical of each approach, using two imaginary companies, Alpha and Beta, that however reflect real, common situations.

The adoption of a more or less rational approach seems to depend not so much on the company's official structure, but more on the nature of the designer (personality, professional maturity and stylistic identity), the managerial philosophy of the manufacturing company, and especially the type of collection being designed, because as we have already seen, more commercial collections have harsh cost restrictions and require a more rational approach.

In the case of an emerging designer, who has a strong personality and tends to work without a team or support structure, the adoption of rational models in collection development is difficult and in any event not suitable for this type of creativity. If, on the other hand, the designer has experience, works with his/her team and is used to collaborating, a rational approach allows for better results in terms of breadth and structure of the collection proposals.

The involvement of the designer also depends on the willingness of the two parties, formally defined in the contract. There are licensing contracts that provide for strict control by the designer. In other cases the licensor itself grants the licensee greater freedom in developing stylistic concepts. American *maisons*, for example, that often depend on Italian licensees, manage their licenses using a model that entails considerable freedom.

Figure 7 The collection development process: a comparison of two models

Distinguishing aspects	Alpha (rational model)	Beta (relational model)
Type of company	• Large size, formal menswear and womenswear, approximately ten licenses and some proprietary brands	• Large size, formal apparel principally for women, various licenses and a proprietary brand
Organizational structures	• At the corporate level, staff functions and 5 divisions (men's, women's, geographic areas) • Women's division: staff functions (purchasing, logistics, marketing, operation, personnel and control), 5 business units per brand • Each business unit has a brand manager, multiple style offices if there are multiple collections	• Some centralized functions and offices dedicated to the single licenses (selection of fabrics and accessories, styles, pattern making and sales)
Process management	• The style offices develop the collections following plans and deadlines agreed on at the corporate level • The designers are continuously pressured to respect deadlines. Designers receive precise indications based on market analysis • There are differences between ready to wear (RTW) collections and diffusion: in RTW there is more stylistic and pattern making research, more prototypes are made, sales are in the showroom. In diffusion, sales are through agents, by which the collection is calibrated, including completion articles	• The company defines general guidelines • Personalized management by the single stylistic offices with respect to the designer and his/her way of working • The *product manager* coordinates the activity, deals with the designer, establishes constraints on the collection, manages times, collaborates in fabric research, and receives sales data • The extraordinary effort by the employees makes up for the designer's failure to meet deadlines
Operating tools and systems	• Market analysis (broad and structured) and preparation of final sales data, collection plans and timing, and control of variety	• Market surveys (focused and occasional), preparation of final sales data

Each manufacturing company (that is a licensee or in any event in charge of product development and production) is also characterized by a managerial philosophy that reflects its history, business values, vocation and the consequent product choices. For example, in high-end women's apparel, the manufacturing company is used to experimenting with more intense creativity, in terms of fashion and materials. When the product is formal menswear, innovation is less pronounced and the adoption of rational approaches is spontaneous.

In general, when a company aims at more commercial market segments, or stylistic research is less daring, it is convenient to use more rational and efficiency-based approaches, for both men's and women's collections. It should be noted though, that nowadays the intensity of competitive pressure requires greater attention regarding the way the process is managed. Many companies, even those with a strong creative spirit, are increasingly oriented towards the rationalization of activities and the adoption of tools for coordination.

From the standpoint of management of the collection development process, we can conclude that, despite taking into account the lack of uniformity between the various situations observed (type of collection, profile of the designer and the manufacturing company), there is room for rationalization and the opportunity for managerial roles that integrate the various competencies in a balanced manner. This orientation is increasingly true and necessary due to the changes described in the first chapter. Each model is more suited to different situations. In particular, the adoption of relational approaches seems more appropriate for situations of stylistic experimentation and development and strengthening of new brands, while the rational approach seems more suited to managing situations with stylistic continuity and exploitation of established brands.

Bibliography

Colucci, M., Montaguti, E., & Lago, U. (2008), "Managing brand extension via licensing: An investigation into the high-end fashion industry", *International Journal of Research in Marketing*, 25(2), pp. 129-137.
Corbellini, E. (2006), "Patrizia Pepe: Advanced Quick Fashion", SDA Bocconi – Case Centre.
Filippetti, S. (2015), "Valentino e la scommessa vinta del Quatar", *Il Sole 24 Ore*, April.
Giannelli, B. & Saviolo, S. (editor, 2001), *Il licensing nel sistema moda. Evoluzione, criticità e prospettive*. Etas, Milan.
Granger, M.M. (2012), *The Fashion Industry and Its Careers*. Bloomsbury, London.
Guercini, S. & Runfola, A. (2010), "Business networks and retail international-

ization: A case analysis in the fashion industry", *Industrial Marketing Management*, 39(6), pp. 908-916.

Rath, P.M., Petrizzi, R., & Gill, P. (2012). *Marketing Fashion. A Global Perspective*. Bloomsbury, London.

Sacchi, M.S. (2010), "Ecco dove producono i big dell'Italian Style", *Corriere della Sera*, 19 October.

Saviolo, S. & Testa, S. (2000), *Le imprese del sistema moda. Il management al servizio della creatività*. Etas, Milan.

Tungate, M. (2008), *Fashion Brands. Branding Style from Armani to Zara*, Kogan-Page, London.

Varacca Capello, P. & Ravasi, D. (2002), "Il rapporto stile-industria: l'esperienza italiana nell'abbigliamento formale di fascia alta", *Economia & Management*, n. 5, pp. 59-75.

3 Collections and the Development Process

by *Flavio Sciuccati and Paola Varacca Capello*

1. The fundamental elements of collections

A collection is an assortment of clothing items and accessories that is conceived, presented and sold in a coordinated way by a company (Varacca Capello, 1993). It represents the seasonal offer of a line. Companies usually do not offer only one line on the market, but rather a portfolio of lines, potentially aimed at different targets with different types of products, in various forms, even if they are joined under one brand (see Box 1, chapter 2). Portfolios of lines pose problems of internal consistency and potential overlapping, that must be solved when the company defines the guidelines (or "brief") of the collection, upstream of development. Overlapping and inconsistency are more frequent for licensed collections, because the creation of models takes place at least in part without the supervision of the company's style office and strong involvement of the licensor's merchandising.

It can be useful to have a portfolio of lines to balance the conflicting needs of maintaining stylistic identity and searching for new concepts. For example, one or more lines can be dedicated to fashion products, with presentations at fashion shows, investments in promotion and high prices. Others, aimed at a broader target, will be balanced in terms of price, style and coverage of customers' functional needs and occasions of use. In other cases, there will be a single line of articles that cover various customer needs, including proposals from previous seasons (see Box 1, regarding Furla).

In this chapter we refer to a single line and thus to the related collections that will be developed during the course of the seasons. In the development of a collection three basic elements converge, the company's more

Box 1. Collections at Furla

Furla is an Italian leather goods brand in the premium segment with global recognition. It identifies and presents itself as "Joyful & Contemporary Italian Lifestyle". In 2014 Furla reached sales of 262 million Euros, and is present in 100 markets with 398 monobrand stores, in addition to 1,100 points of sale in multibrand stores and international department stores. The company has 1,185 employees, of a hundred different nationalities.

Despite leather remaining its core business (especially bags, and then small leather goods and footwear), Furla stores offer a range of articles from textile accessories to jewels, watches, umbrellas and glasses. For some of these categories licensing agreements have been signed with top Italian companies. Starting in June 2015, menswear was introduced with the 2015 FW collection, presented at Pitti.

In leather goods there are four collections each year: pre-fall, fall, cruise, and main SS. Deliveries occur monthly, with the following schedule: pre-fall in May, June and July; fall in August, September and October; cruise in November, December and January; main SS in February, March and April. Each season proposes approximately 900 SKUs (that refer to model, material and color). Each season is divided into a certain number of lines (less than 15 for pre, approximately 20-25 for main). The lines share a certain stylistic concept. Collections are the same for all markets, although some local needs are considered (in particular for the size and colors of bags).

In addition to these collections there are 4-5 capsules per year, mini collections consisting of bags and accessories created for specific occasions (for example Mother's Day and Valentine's Day).

In the construction of collections the factors considered are price segment, functions (i.e. the type of bag: shoulder, backpack, handle bag, shopping bag, etc.), the occasions of use (elegant, casual, ceremony, daytime, etc.), targeted to both mature customers and young and very young customers: "99 out of 100 women must like our collection!"

From a stylistic standpoint Furla products stand out for their clean lines, femininity, character, simplicity and fashion content. Each collection includes both new products and ongoing products, which are renewed each season as regards details, colors and materials. The brand has had international success thanks in part to the launch of highly successful products, such as the iconic Candy Bag, a PVC satchel, subsequently paired with materials such as leather and cane. The Candy Bag was followed by the Furla Metropolis bag, produced in various sizes, and available in many different colors and materials.

Source: based on information from the company.

or less explicit and rational consideration of which determines the efficacy of the proposal and the response from customers (Figure 1):

- market positioning and target;
- stylistic identity;
- collection structure.

Figure 1 The development of collections: fundamental elements

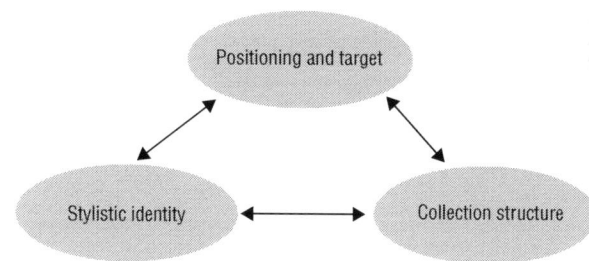

a) *Market positioning and target.* A collection is aimed at a certain segment of consumers (target), whose needs, tastes and habits constitute the starting point for the development process. The characteristics of a collection as perceived by customers (the fashion content, price range, product categories, combination between products, etc.), determine its positioning with respect to competitors' collections. The positioning chosen is crucial to define the sales offer, especially for entirely new collections, which the company uses to enter a product category for the first time (for example, women's clothing for a company specialized in menswear) or a price segment (for example, the "accessible" lines offered by *maisons* to customers with lower spending capacity). For existing brands or lines, on the other hand, it is critical to monitor the consistency of collections with the acquired position and the dynamics of the target's tastes; or, if this positioning is considered unsatisfactory, how to improve it in light of competitors' offers and the direction of the market.

b) *Stylistic identity.* Each brand and each designer has a precise stylistic identity, that the collection interprets according to the new trends they wish to propose (Corbellini & Saviolo, 2009). For example, Missoni is known for its colored sweaters with subtle lines and zigzag patterns, that are combined and varied in increasingly diverse combinations. Desigual recalls the Mediterranean, with bright prints, colored spots and patterns that are inspired by graffiti culture. Stella McCartney is defined by the characteristic use of certain materials (chains, eco-leather). Some brands link their stylistic identity to single iconic products (Chanel's tweed tailleur), to unchanging formal elements presented repeatedly in various articles and collections (Armani's unstructured jackets) or so-called brand identifiers, such as elements of the logo (Gucci's double G) or groups of colors (green-red-green stripes, again in Gucci).

The development of collections must balance the defense of the brand's stylistic identity with the need to follow trends. The prevalence of one aspect or the other is linked to the desired positioning. Some companies attempt to offer permanent aesthetic values, positioning themselves in exclusive or premium market segments, where maintaining stylistic identity prevails; others, that are characterized by a strong fashion content, will be more flexible and variable in interpreting their stylistic identity.

c) *Collection structure*. The structure of the single collection is given first of all by two variables.

- *Breadth*, measured by the number of SKUs included in the collection. It should be noted that the concept of *Stock Keeping Unit*, that originated in the logistics area, is interpreted differently by companies as a function of the different product categories (clothing, accessories, leather goods, etc.). Sometimes the calculation of SKUs is limited to model/fabric/color combinations, such that model X with cotton fabric and yellow color, for example, represents a single SKU. Other times the calculation includes sizes, generating 4 different SKUs if model X in yellow cotton is produced in small, medium, large and extra-large. In addition to being a "reference", the term SKU can also be translated as "article" or "sale option".

- *Variety*, that depends on the number of product categories that make up the collection. This variable differentiates specialty collections (such as a collection of shirts) from those that include models in multiple categories. When models are coordinated, and maybe they extend to shoes and accessories, we speak of 'total look' collections. The variety determines the breadth, but only to a certain extent, because specialty collections with a vast selection of sizes and colors can generate many SKUs. Just think of t-shirt or polo collections (Lacoste, for example). To the contrary, collections with many product categories can provide a limited selection of models, colors and sizes.

From a broader perspective, variety must be evaluated considering that each article is associated with a data sheet and a bill of materials that list the elements necessary for manufacturing the article: these are stylistic accessories (linings, buttons, threads for outer seams, labels, etc.) and technical accessories (labels, shoulder pads, threads for inner seams, etc.). These elements, that can be more or less numerous, contribute to intensifying variety (Bini, 2011). If we look from the standpoint of production, variety also extends to the types of processes required (the various phases of cutting, manufacturing and finishing of the article), the different manufacturing methods adopted in the factory or in external workshops (work times and cycles, supporting technical documentation, quality procedures) and the related equipment (cutting templates, references in the sewing phase, etc.). These aspects of variety are important because they influence the technical complexity and overall costs that the collection produces (Sciuccati & Varacca Capello, 1999).

Given a certain size (breadth and variety), a collection presents additional *distinguishing characteristics*:

- *the number of events/presentations and deliveries*: there was a time when companies that operated following the *programmato* logic offered two collections a year (one for SS and one for FW), potentially enriched by some 'flash' items. With the internationalization of sales (especially in the North American market, where clients wanted early deliveries), and under pressure from fast fashion, many companies began to divide each seasonal collection into a pre-season and a main-season, with separate deliveries; they later further divided the collections, with a growing convergence between *programmato* and fast fashion;
- *the logics of presentation and sales*: the collection articles can be grouped in different ways at the time of presentation to clients: by themes, colors, combinations, etc. Single articles can also be presented (in *haute couture*, for example). Groups of articles must be consistent from the standpoint of the offer, and suitable for the spaces available to retailers. The logics of presentation thus correspond to the sales packages or modules and the delivery times;

- *functions and occasions of use*: function is a product's ability to satisfy a specific need (for example, an evening gown); the occasion is the time when a certain item/accessory is generally used (for example, beachwear). Both can identify a particular collection or define the internal division;
- *targets*: a collection is usually aimed at a specific segment (men, women, children, or other smaller groups), but can also be divided into products aimed at different segments;
- *price segments*: within each collection there can be various price segments, even in the context of a positioning that has been defined in advance.

The last variable that characterizes collections and conditions their development process is *innovation*, that is, how and to what extent the articles in the collection differ from previous articles (see Figure 2 for a summary). The renewal of collection products does not have specific frequencies, except in *haute couture*, in which every collection is entirely new. They are divided as follows:

- *basic* and *running* (on going) articles, that remain in the collection for multiple seasons. The expression *carry over* is used in this sector, especially for accessory categories, to indicate the articles that are maintained in the subsequent season or for multiple seasons to prolong the life cycle as much as possible;
- *seasonal* articles, that are new and characterize a collection;
- *special* articles (or *limited series*), products that have the purpose of promoting a certain event, for example, like an exhibit or the opening of a new store; or articles included in a collection to meet the needs of specific customers or markets; or also limited editions with special materials or manufacturing methods;
- *capsule collections* dedicated to a certain theme or produced in collaboration with an external designer, that remain on sale only for a short time.

An additional category of articles consists of *never out of stock* (NOOS, also called "permanent"), that must always be available in stock, to be delivered rapidly. They can be ongoing, but also seasonal articles for which regular sales must be ensured (through production launches on forecasts, management of stock products and quick reassortment times at stores).

The degree of innovation changes as a function of the model and materials used. There are articles for which the model is maintained and the materials change (or vice versa), completely new articles in which both are innovated, articles that undergo small changes to the model and/or materials, and others that remain identical with only a change in color.

Innovation is indispensable in fashion companies, but requires a series of activities that, if not adequately managed, translate into greater complexity and thus a loss of operational efficiency (Richetti & Cietta, 2006). Innovations that are the result of purely creative stimuli, without planning the resulting activities, or that are introduced without considering the actual requests from the market, are often unproductive or in any event useful only for communication purposes.

Figure 2 Key factors of a collection

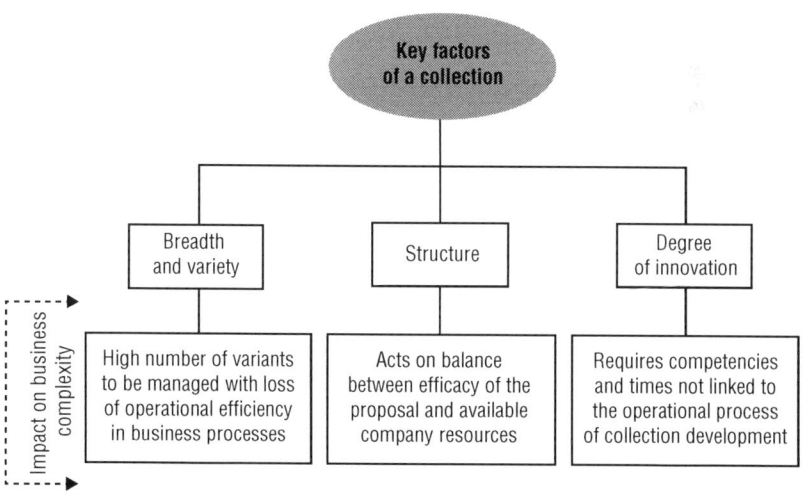

Source: adapted from Sciuccati & Varacca Capello (1999, p. 77)

2. Timing and activities (collection timing)

The operational activities of the fashion sector are dictated by seasons. Appointments with the market are marked by fairs and fashion shows. Delivery of the product to stores is determined by specific deadlines. To be on time for these appointments and deadlines, a fashion company is obliged to plan its activities with a well-structured operating cycle, scheduling activities working backward from the appointments (retro-planning), as shown in Figure 3.

The chart refers to a company that operates principally through the wholesale channel and structures its collections with a single seasonal offer. If we consider SS, the items must be delivered to stores starting in January (but there could be deliveries already at the end of November/start of December for some global markets that start much earlier than Europe). The production of garments (according to the *programmato* model) starts after the sales campaign and the collection of the order portfolio are completed. The presentation of the seasonal proposal to retailers and distributors, that marks the start of the campaign, takes place around June/July for men's collections and September for women's collections. To present the collections on those dates, development starts in January/February (if not already in December, in many cases) including through a detailed analysis of the sales data for the previous SS season. Where there are directly managed stores, companies also use recent sales data and current data for the FW season (simultaneously with the development of the SS collection), especially for ongoing themes that cut across seasons. In March the actual creation phase begins.

If we look at the supply chain and the production of fabrics (Redaelli & Rubertelli, 2009), times are longer. Fabrics are presented at fairs in January or February. Thus fabric suppliers will have worked on the development of their collections in the final months of the previous year.

Reassortment takes place during the season. At the end of the season, after the end-of-season sales, the goods remaining in stock at the stores (whether proprietary or not) can be withdrawn and allocated to various channels, such as outlets.

The collection cycle, from the first phases of development until the closing of sales to final consumers, lasts at least 18 months.

3 COLLECTIONS AND THE DEVELOPMENT PROCESS 59

Figure 3 Cycle of SS and FW collections

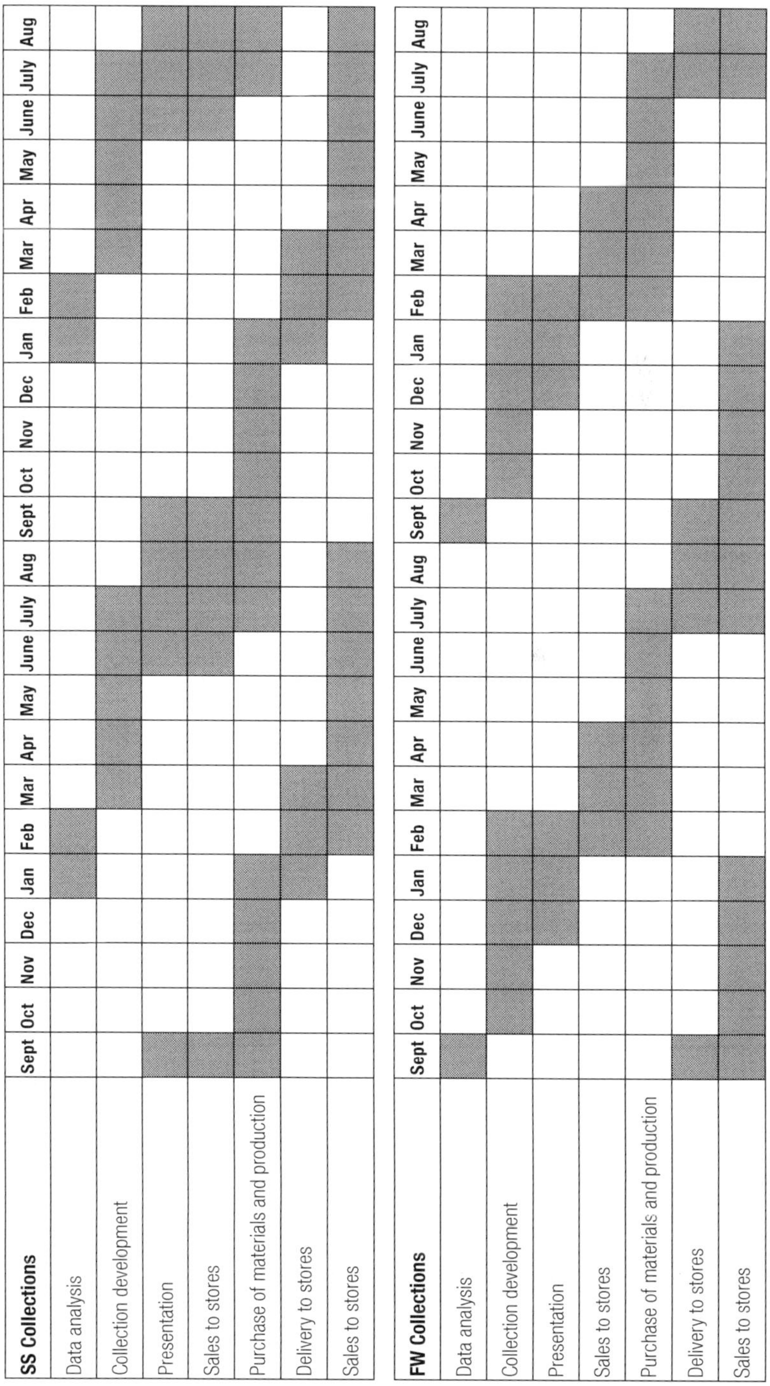

SS Collections	Sept	Oct	Nov	Dec	Jan	Feb	Mar	Apr	May	June	July	Aug	Sept	Oct	Nov	Dec	Jan	Feb	Mar	Apr	May	June	July	Aug
Data analysis					▓																			
Collection development			▓	▓	▓	▓	▓																	
Presentation																								
Sales to stores		▓																						
Purchase of materials and production					▓			▓	▓															
Delivery to stores							▓																	
Sales to stores																								

FW Collections	Sept	Oct	Nov	Dec	Jan	Feb	Mar	Apr	May	June	July	Aug	Sept	Oct	Nov	Dec	Jan	Feb	Mar	Apr	May	June	July	Aug
Data analysis	▓																							
Collection development											▓	▓	▓											
Presentation									▓															
Sales to stores													▓											
Purchase of materials and production															▓	▓	▓							
Delivery to stores																							▓	
Sales to stores																								

This phenomenon has various implications:

- the collection is designed, sold and produced well in advance of the time when the end consumer will be able to buy it;
- the cost and revenue flow generated by a collection is not limited to one accounting period; this creates accounting problems regarding accrual, planning and control;
- fashion companies are simultaneously involved in a certain number of collections in different phases, with problems of coordination and overlapping of activities.

As mentioned in Chapter 1, the traditional *programmato* model with one collection per season is for the most part obsolete, and fashion companies are facing important changes:

- the transformation of seasonal offers from one to multiple collections;
- the development of collections with the sell-in moment closer and closer to the sell-out moment (reduction of lead time and time to market). The most recent trend is that of brands that make some articles available right after the fashion show, in online stores or selected stores (see Box 2, regarding Moschino);
- the parallel management of wholesale and retail and the preparation of packages or offer plans destined only to retail, with repeat deliveries during the season to guarantee constant product availability for its DOS and avoid lack of selection in stores that would damage the brand's image with end consumers;
- the need to meet differentiated international needs. Consider the launch periods of the collections on different markets. In the United States and Northern Europe the SS collection is sent to stores in mid-November, while in Southern Europe the launch is in January. The need for early deliveries can be resolved with specific production activities for foreign markets.

This work on the offer increases the complexity of collections, making the structure of operational timing increasingly complex and customized for each company. In addition, the seasonal schedules lead to the overlapping of one season with another, including in the simple case of one collection per season. In figure 3 we see that at different times of the year the company is working on the SS collection and the FW collection at the same time, even if the functions occupy different activities. If, for example, we consider January, the activities the company needs to carry out for a men's collection are as follows:

1. the FW collection is in the presentation and sell-in phase;
2. the SS season is in the phase of delivery and invoicing to trade (retailers), while the production phase is coming to an end;
3. trade is closing sales with end-of-season sales of FW collections. If the company is in retail, it is already picking up seasonal returns from its stores;
4. outlets must be supplied with the returns from the previous season (or in some cases with special production items), that are placed into shipment;
5. the development of the new SS collection is launched. The style office and product directors are working to design the offer.

If the company alternates the scheduled offer with collections to be sold in season, in the sell-in phases the company simultaneously presents:
- a *programmato* collection for delivery in the next six months (in July the SS collection for January delivery);
- a ready collection for immediate delivery (in July a FW winter collection to be shipped as soon as possible).

This overlapping of activities with rhythms that can be very differentiated and frenetic, has a strong impact on organization and leads to two necessities:
- it is necessary to define the operating times in a detailed manner and set times for verifying the progress of activities, as well as deadlines by which certain activities must be completed. For example, a time must be set when the collection will be "frozen" and it will no longer be possible to add fabrics or new models (to have the possibility to order materials in advance as needed);
- the collaborators must be able to work in multifunctional teams; the activity of each function is to be classified in an overall plan, because each activity heavily influences the performance of the others.

Box 2. Moschino and the "Next Day After the Runway"

> Moschino occupies a prominent place on the international fashion scene, thanks to its history and stylistic continuity. The three lines in which Moschino's offering is divided ("Couture!", "Boutique Moschino" and "Love Moschino", the latter licensed to SINV) offer different types of products, the expression of a creative capacity that through the reinterpretation of classics, makes irony and elegance its strong points. The first line is presented following a specific calendar: in February the FW Moschino women's collection is shown, and in September the SS Moschino women's collection is shown.
> All of the lines have undergone a repositioning towards a higher fashion content, thanks also to the entry of Jeremy Scott as the new creative director. The American designer, who grew up professionally between Paris and Los Angeles, has been able to successfully develop the *griffe*, including expanding the offer of accessories. In fact, the strategy entails a growing emphasis on men's collections, greater attention to accessories (not only "leather" but also technology) and a review of seasonal schedules, that is linked to the development of digital, which the brand wants to strengthen. In this direction Moschino has presented itself as an innovative brand precisely from the standpoint of integration between sales in stores, digital communication and e-commerce.
> In February 2014 a capsule collection was launched, "Fast Fashion – Next Day After the Runway", that was immediately made available in Moschino's online stores and at some selected stores (such as Colette and 10 Corso Como). The collection included ten articles worn in the 2014-2015 FW fashion show. The same approach was then adopted for the September show, that presented twenty-eight pieces with the Barbie theme, including backpacks, iPhone covers, a miniskirt and t-shirts, that were made available immediately after the fashion show. In February 2015 a capsule collection was launched with the "Ready to Bear" label, again sold in Moschino's online store right after launch. The capsule collection for FW 2015-2016 was also available the next day in the brand's main boutiques in Milan, Rome, London, Paris and Los Angeles, at Moschino's franchisee network and in the most prestigious international multibrand stores, including Net-A-Porter, Opening Ceremony and Luisaviaroma.

Source: based on information from the company.

Companies that structure their offers according to the fast fashion logic obviously have collection structures and delivery times that are very different (and diversified depending on the operators): the Inditex group excels in frequent reassortments and constant deliveries of new articles to its stores (see Box 3).

Box 3. The Inditex group and fast fashion

The main characteristic of Inditex's business model is the speed of the production cycle, that guarantees flexibility and allows for adapting products to clients' needs. The entire process, from design to delivery of the articles, lasts on average between two and three weeks; for direct competitors, such as H&M, it takes at least six weeks. The model is based on production in small batches; less than 25% of the offer is planned before the season. The rest is created and produced during the season, reserving between 50 and 60 percent of production capacity of outside suppliers in advance.
The group has a high degree of integration both upstream and downstream. The development process starts in the store. The assortment is created by the designers based on what consumers want. The store managers monitor customer reaction, in particular which articles are purchased or not, in addition to information asked of the sales staff. Every day the store manager reports this information to headquarters, where market specialists (the "sales" staff) process the inputs and transmit them to 250 internal designers, who rapidly develop the new ideas and send sketches to manufacturing.
The group's production is located for the most part in its own factories or at contractors close to the main facilities (in Portugal, Morocco and Turkey). When the items are finished, they are sent to the laboratories for ironing and quality control. Lastly, they are sent to the central warehouses. The group manages nine logistical centers in Spain (specialized by brand, and in some cases, by product category). All of the production is sent to these centers and then shipped to the local platforms in the destination countries, that transfer them to stores. Recently, logistical platforms have been created in Asia (Israel, Japan and South Korea) and in Europe (Turkey and France). Each store in the world receives reassortments and new articles twice a week. The product goes from the logistical centers to European stores in 24-36 hours, and to other stores around the world in 48 hours.

Source: Lojacono, Misani, & Varacca Capello (2013).

3. Activities in the collection development process

The collection development process is made up of many activities, assigned to various offices and persons who interact with each other. The activities to be carried out and the corresponding organizational roles depend on the characteristics of the company that develops the collections, or those of its partners, in particular the licensees and suppliers of finished products. To provide an initial, simplified view, these activities can be divided into four phases.

1. *Formulation of collection guidelines.* This phase starts with an analysis of the final figures for the previous collections and a market analysis of clients and suppliers, in terms of competition. This information is useful to define the structure of the new collection (maintain or modify with respect to the past) and indicate any potential stylistic references. In other words, the development of new collections must start with quantitative briefs and potentially stylistic briefs, so that the search for fabrics, accessories, work processes and models is oriented in the right direction. General goals must be defined regarding what the collection is to include: targets and markets, products, price segments, style and offer options, and level of complexity.
2. *Collection planning (merchandising and timing).* The merchandising plan defines the offer on a quantitative level, indicating the division of the SKUs that it will include, the division of the collections based on the variables considered most important (product categories, basic vs. fashion, new items, etc.) and the structure foreseen for industrial costs and prices (Donnellan, 2014). The timing consists of temporal planning of the activities to be carried out through the definition of a calendar in which the most critical points of decision are highlighted.
3. *Executive development of the collection (prototyping, samples and industrialization).* This phase entails a part with research on materials, fabrics and accessories, stylistic research, pattern making, prototypes and tests, up to the final definition of the collection and samples (editing). On the other hand there is the industrialization, that exactly defines the characteristics of the articles for industrial production (listed in the data sheet and the bill of materials), the materials to be ordered, and if the company produces internally, the commitment of resources and productive capacity. These parts of the executive development are connected but require different competencies: specific activities, in particular those relating to industrialization, can be delegated to finished product suppliers.
4. *Presentation of the collection.* This involves the presentation of all of the material to support the promotion activities and showroom sales, including the fashion show (Jackson & Shaw, 2006).

Until a few years ago, companies concentrated in particular on executive development, while now many pay more attention to the first two phases as well (guidelines and planning), because they understand that development must be organized rationally in order to produce the desired results in terms of quantity, times and costs. In the past, guidelines and planning were carried out implicitly and the success of the collection depended greatly on the experience of the product and the relational skills of the people who held management roles. The task of coordination was historically carried out by the so-called *uomo/donna prodotto* (product manager). When licensing contracts began to become common, this figure became responsible for the development of the collection, coordination between the offices (style, pattern making, sales and marketing), and at times research on fabrics and accessories.

Figure 4 describes how some well-known Italian companies divide the phases of development of RTW apparel collections between internal and external partners. Two chapters are dedicated to the phase of defining the guidelines and the instrument of the merchandising plan (Chapters 5 and 6). Planning, executive development and the presentation of the collection are described briefly here and taken up again in Chapter 7, dedicated to the critical aspects of the process.

Figure 4 Outsourcing choices in collection development

	Design	Prototypes	Samples	Industrializ.	Production
Company A	●	◐	○	◐	○
Company B	●	●	○	●	○
Company C	●	●	◐	●	◐
Company D	●	●	●	●	●
Company E	●	●	○	●	○
Company F	●	●	○	●	○
Company G	●	●	○	●	○
Company H	●	●	○	●	○
Company I	●	◐	○	◐	○
Company L	●	●	○	●	○

The information refers in particular to casual and sport collections.
● 100% internal; ○ 100% external; ◐ internal and external.

Source: prepared by Flavio Sciuccati.

3.1 *The planning of a collection*

The planning of the collection development activities requires above all their precise identification. The nature of these activities depends in part on the type of collection; for example, commercial collections require cost checks before decisions on the items to include or exclude from the samples.

The definition of the activities also demands identifying the people responsible for their performance and drawing up a calendar. The calendar is obtained by working backwards from the scheduled dates (for example the fashion show) and sequencing the activities such that the calendar contains all of them. It is also necessary to identify the moments when certain decisions must be made. Figure 5 describes the phases of development of collections of a large company that produces casual garments. Note the presence of critical moments, like the closing of orders, that cannot be postponed, because they would cause serious delays in the subsequent activities.

A common error is to define the calendar without adequately considering the workloads originating from the size, structure and innovation of the collection. In this sense, the merchandising plan is the tool that allows for quantifying the effort for designing the collection and introducing project management logics in fashion as well. It is true that product development times are not easy to schedule. For example, it is not possible to predict how many passages through pattern making the development of a new model will require. It is possible, however, to estimate an average number of passages for articles of a certain type and to calculate the foreseeable use of production capacity, based on experience from previous seasons. On the importance that merchandising plays in collection development, see the example in Box 4, regarding Balenciaga.

Fashion companies with less propensity for planning can compensate for these problems with the flexibility and talent of the people dedicated to developing the collection. In addition, the aesthetic and intrinsic qualities of products remain central in this sector, and can win out over inefficiencies and delays due to lack of planning. Nevertheless, the analysis, prediction and quantification of development activities allow for more rational management of each activity, and thus better results.

Box 4 Merchandising at Balenciaga

The French designer Nicolas Ghesquière was the creative director at Balenciaga from 1997 to 2012. After leaving the company he gave an interview in which he confessed his displeasure with how the historic Parisian maison was managed.
"I was the one who introduced the concept of being commercial at Balenciaga. I wanted to do it from the beginning, but the group that owned the *maison* at the time didn't have this idea. There wasn't even a product team. There was nothing".
"The last two or three years were continuous frustration. The strongest items in the fashion shows were ignored by the managers. They didn't realize that to have that nice leather jacket that sold easily it was necessary to go through a technically sophisticated model to be presented at the shows. I began to be unhappy when I realized that there was no consideration, interest or recognition for the research I had done; they only worried about what the final product for sale would be like. This short-sighted desire meant forgetting that all of the most popular current items came from collections that we designed ten years ago. They became classics and continue to be so. Even if the shows were extremely rich in ideas and products, there was no subsequent merchandising. With a single jacket we could have launched entire commercial strategies. I would have liked to do it, but I couldn't do everything myself. I divided my time between designs for fashion shows and commercial models - I became Mr. Merchandiser. There has never been a merchandiser at Balenciaga, which I regret terribly".

Source: Ciaravella (2013), abridged from.

3.2 Executive development

3.2.1 Prototyping and samples

The activities necessary to prepare the collection samples consist of stylistic research and pattern making, the creation of prototypes and the definition of the collection. The prototypes can be made in continuous fabrics or fabrics already in stock (canvas was used in the past), to then move on to fabrics that have similar weights and characteristics to those to be used in the new collection.

The prototypes are tried by models. With a series of fittings and adjustments, that can go from one to four or five based on the level of innovation and complexity of the garment, the final prototype is developed. At this point the collection is decided by the management or the office with the last word, that varies from company to company. The collection will

Figure 5 Calendar of collections in a large casual company

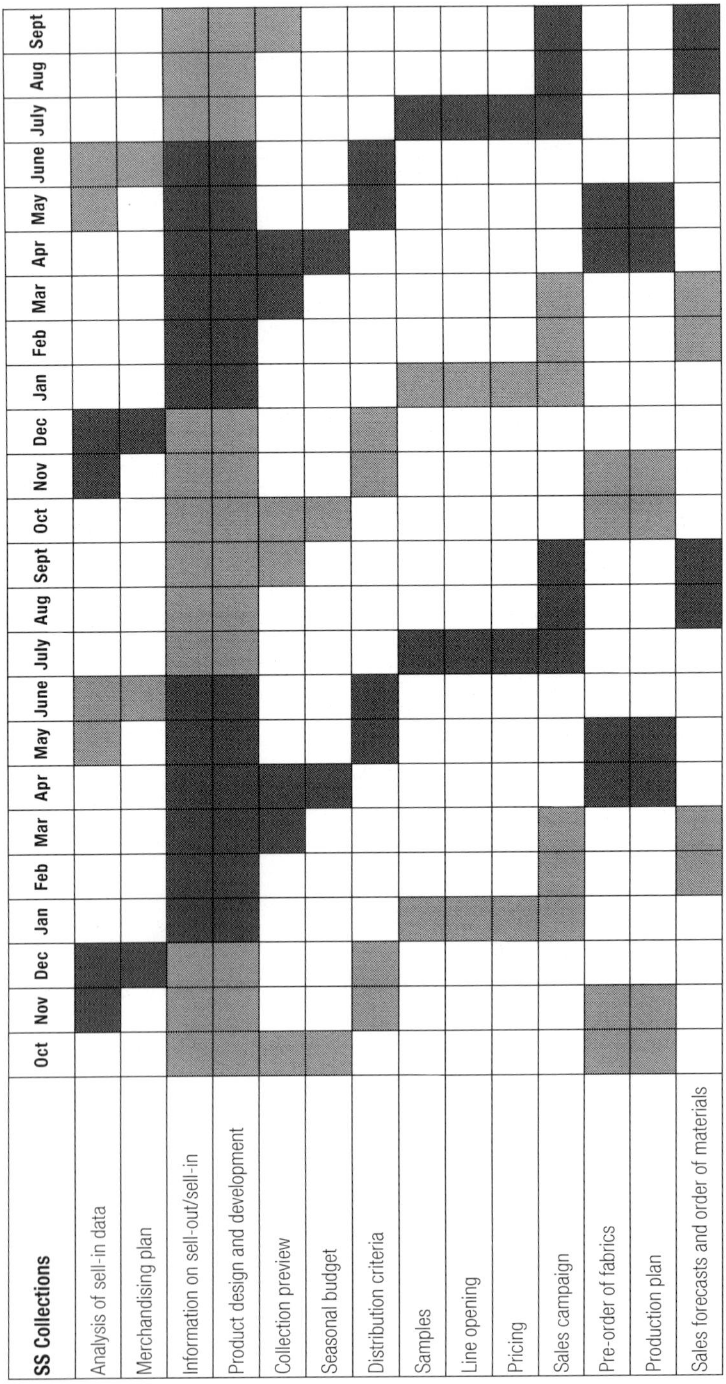

SS Collections	Oct	Nov	Dec	Jan	Feb	Mar	Apr	May	June	July	Aug	Sept	Oct	Nov	Dec	Jan	Feb	Mar	Apr	May	June	July	Aug	Sept
Analysis of sell-in data		■																						
Merchandising plan			■																					
Information on sell-out/sell-in		■	■																					
Product design and development					■	■	■	■																
Collection preview								■																
Seasonal budget									■															
Distribution criteria										■														
Samples										■	■	■												
Line opening												■												
Pricing													■											
Sales campaign												■	■	■	■	■								
Pre-order of fabrics															■									
Production plan																	■							
Sales forecasts and order of materials																	■	■						

3   COLLECTIONS AND THE DEVELOPMENT PROCESS

SS Collections	Oct	Nov	Dec	Jan	Feb	Mar	Apr	May	June	July	Aug	Sept	Oct	Nov	Dec	Jan	Feb	Mar	Apr	May	June	July	Aug	Sept
Production orders		■	■	■	■	■		■	■	■	■	■												
Final sales	■						▨						■						▨					
Closing of production orders							▨												▨					
SS production				■	■	■	▨	▨	▨	▨	▨	■				■	■	■	▨	▨	▨	▨	▨	■
FW production								▨	▨	▨	▨									▨	▨	▨	▨	
Warehouse plan and priority						▨				▨	▨							▨				▨	▨	
Deliveries to stores		■						▨	▨					■						▨	▨			
Proceeds from stores FW			■	■	■	■	■	▨			▨	▨			■	■	■	■	■	▨			▨	▨
Proceeds from stores SS									■	■	■	■									■	■	■	■

FW ■
SS ▨

generally contain a smaller number of styles than the series of prototypes developed (see Figure 6).

Downstream of the definition of the collection the sample set is produced, which represents a more or less complete assortment of all of the articles, generally produced in only one size and one color. The samples are used for presentation to clients and for photo shoots. More than one unit is generally produced (copies or repeats), depending on the markets and agents. The company often has specialized internal or external laboratories for the production of samples.

To shorten times, today companies tend to avoid initial prototyping with canvas if possible (or bonded leather for bags) and immediately try the materials that will then be used in the collection. Computerized design systems (CAD), that are increasingly common, and the continuous reduction of lead times by suppliers, are facilitating this progress.

3.2.2 Industrialization

When the collection is defined, the prototypes are subject to calculation and technical checks to transform them into garments that can be produced industrially. This phase also allows for defining the precise industrial cost of each SKU. Often, and especially for more commercial collections, the verification of economic feasibility takes place in the previous phases and

Figure 6 Breadth of collections in the development phases

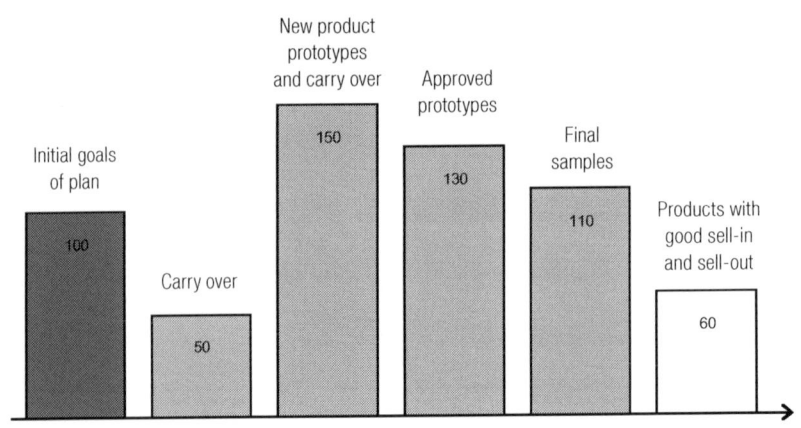

The graph refers to a simplified collection of 100 articles.

thus comes before the definition of the collection. Industrialization thus consists of four main phases:

1. the production of the *sample garment*, i.e. the final sample, that is used as reference for production, and the compilation of the data sheets and bill of materials;
2. size development;
3. the placing of fabrics;
4. the development of equipment (cutting templates, cartoons, etc.).

When development is internal and production is external, companies give suppliers an industrialization package with specifications and all of the supporting materials. The use of external contractors is also increasingly common for prototyping. Outsourcing is partial when companies prefer to continue to develop their most important and complex garments themselves.

Given that fabrics (and materials in general) are an important factor of innovation nowadays, it is useful to also involve suppliers in the research or development of exclusive *ad hoc* materials starting with the initial research phases. In the case of *ad hoc* materials, specific activities are required (briefs, prototypes, samples) that increase the workload of the style offices and the product directors. So if these activities are not planned, they can delay the development of the collection and the start of production.

3.3 *Presentation of the collection*

The collection (or part of it, when there are multiple occasions for presentation, as often happens) can be presented to the public in various locations:

- in the shows during Fashion weeks, where the most prestigious apparel *griffes* participate;
- in fairs and exhibitions. The best-known are those involving materials (yarns and fabrics are presented in Italy at MilanoUnica), accessories and those specialized in certain product categories (wedding dresses, for example);
- in showrooms (at companies or managed directly by the agent responsible for a certain geographic area);
- privately (for strategic clients, such as American department stores).

The presentation of the collection assumes the preparation of supporting materials, from color schemes to the presentation of outfits. Marketing and sales are responsible for this phase, but style offices and product directors have a crucial role in developing the design of the collection, i.e. in presenting the themes and articles of the collection in a thought-out way, and choosing the looks that will be used in the shows, in coordination with the communication activities. As an example see Box 5, relating to the sales campaign of Fausto Puglisi.

Box 5. The sales campaign of Fausto Puglisi

Fausto Puglisi is one of the most important Italian designers. Clients include approximately 150 stores or department stores, which include the most important clients at the national and international level. The seasonal proposal is divided into various collections, for men's (four per year: main and fashion show, for the two seasons) and women's (four per year: pre-fall, fashion show, resort and fashion show). The sales campaigns follow this calendar: articles are delivered to stores after approximately 5 months.

Month	Shows	Sales campaign
January	Men's	FW Man Main and Fashion Show (continues until mid-February).
		SS Ladies Pre-fall (continues until mid-February) and makes up approximately 60%-70% of sales for the season
February		FW Man Main and Fashion Show
		FW Ladies Pre-fall
		FW Ladies Fashion Show: starts in the second half of the month and lasts until mid-March
March	Women's	FW Ladies Fashion Show
April		
May		
June	Men's	PE Man Main and Fashion Show (continues until mid-July)
		PE Ladies Resort (continues until mid-July) and makes up approximately 60%-70% of sales for the season
July		PE Man Main and Fashion Show
		PE Ladies Resort
August		
September	Women's	PE Ladies Fashion Show: starts in the second half of the month and lasts until mid-October
October		PE Ladies Fashion Show
November		
December		

> The collections are divided by themes (colors, prints, styles) and occasions of use (ceremonies/evening, cocktails, daytime and recently, casual). For women the main collections (pre-fall and resort) present about 120-150 articles, while the fashion shows have fewer items. Approximately 30 releases are carried out. The sales campaign takes place in the Milan showroom.
> Not all of the articles in the collection are presented in all of the color variants (never more than two or three). To show the different combinations, the sales personnel prepares the look book that shows the pictures of the garments worn by models in all of the variants paired with data sheets (line sheets and color cards) that provide details on the materials, the color variants and the product codes. The sellers have a binder with the press review on the items in the collection and on the fashion show. The choice of which variants will be visible in the showroom is critical, because those are the ones that sell the most, both because they are suggested by the brand, and due to the effect of seeing and touching them. To support sales, events are organized in the most important stores (trunk shows), inviting the most loyal clients, and if possible with the participation of Franco Puglisi himself.
> Brief training courses are also organized to explain the seasonal proposals to the sales staff in stores (especially at department stores), highlighting conceptual and style aspects, but also technical details. The sales campaign makes use of freelance store assistants, a common practice for the most established brands. Before the start of the sales campaign the client lists are examined to draw up a budget, aimed above all at launching the orders for fabrics and developing a forecast of sales volumes.
> The analysis of the data from the first two weeks of sale is very important, to proceed to make any adjustments to the seasonal proposal. Gathering feedback from the sales assistants is also critical and very useful, organized by models, fabrics and requests for upcoming seasons.

Source: based on company information.

Bibliography

Bini, V. (2011), *La supply chain nella moda*, FrancoAngeli, Milan.
Ciaravella, M. (2013), "Parla Nicolas Ghesquière: ho lasciato Balenciaga perché il management non capisce la moda", *Corriere della Sera Style*, May 23, http://style.corriere.it/blog-michele-ciavarella/2013/05/23/nicolas-ghesquiere-ho-lasciato-balenciaga-perche-il-management-non-capisce-la-moda/.
Corbellini, E. & Saviolo, S. (2009), *Managing Fashion and Luxury Companies*, Etas, Milan.
Donnellan, J. (2014), *Merchandise Buying and Management*. Bloomsbury, London.

Jackson, T. & Shaw, D. (2006), *The Fashion Handbook*, Routledge, London.
Lojacono, G., Misani, N., & Varacca Capello, P. (2014), "The International Growth of Fast Fashion Retailers: the Inditex Case", SDA Bocconi – Case Centre.
Redaelli, E. & Rubertelli, M. (2009), *Design del prodotto moda. Dal tessuto alla passerella*. FrancoAngeli, Milan.
Ricchetti, M. & Cietta, E. (2006), *Il valore della moda. Industria e servizi in un settore guidato dall'innovazione*. Bruno Mondadori, Milan.
Sciuccati, F. M. & Varacca Capello, P. (1999), "Il sistema moda e la gestione della varietà", *Economia & Management*, 5, pp. 57-72.
Varacca Capello, P. (1993), "Lo sviluppo delle collezioni nel sistema moda. Logiche e strumenti operativi", *Economia & Management*, 6, pp. 86-97.

4 Fashion Trends

by *Diego Rinallo*

1. Fashion trends and collection development

In the clothing world innovation is driven more by style than by technology (Cappetta, Cillo, & Ponti, 2006; Hirschmann, 1986; Rinallo, Golfetto, & Gibbert, 2006). In other words, it is linked principally to the aesthetic and symbolic aspects of products. Consumers usually choose a fashion product when it appeals to their senses and/or is able to communicate aspects of their identity and belonging to certain peer groups. In many cases, the presence of functional performance is taken for granted, and does not represent an important preference factor. In that context, knowledge of prevailing fashion trends at a given time is a very important asset that allows for limiting the risk of innovations that are incompatible with those developed by competitors and complementary manufacturers.

In the development of new collections, textile and clothing companies must in fact deal with problems of modularity. That is, consumers must be able to pair clothes and accessories produced by different manufacturers. For example, flared trousers assume certain types of shoes; boots, jeans of a certain length and cut in a certain way; green goes well with certain colors, and not others; and so forth. The textile and clothing supply chain is also very fragmented. It is made up of many small, highly-specialized companies. Thus, unlike what happens in technological sectors, that are usually more concentrated, no company is big enough to impose its innovations as the standard to which competitors and producers of complementary products must adapt.

Box 1. An example of a macro-trend in men's consumption: The metrosexual

In recent decades, there have been numerous attempts by companies, media and communications agencies to "convert" Western men to consumption styles based on greater awareness of their own physical appearance. For centuries, the ethic of masculinity has been linked more to doing, than appearing. The search for beauty, considered legitimate for women, has thus been suspect when men act the same way. The first attempts to overcome this cultural taboo date back to the 1980s, when certain lifestyle magazines in the English-speaking world aimed at men proposed the idea of a *new man* to their readers (and advertisers), a man more in touch with his feminine side and eager to care for his own physical appearance. Many consumers did not find it easy to identify with this model, and in the 90s other magazines reacted by proposing a *new lad*, a rougher man (to the point of machismo) dedicated to more traditionally male interests (sports, automobiles, alcohol). At the start of the new millennium, history repeated itself with the media sensation sparked by the so-called *metrosexual*. The term was initially coined by the journalist Mark Simpson to refer to male consumers who live in large cities or close to them, who invest a significant amount of time and money to care for their physical appearance, and despite usually being heterosexual, tend to adopt the aesthetic sensitivity associated with gay men (Simpson, 1994; 2003). Men such as the soccer player David Beckham, with his unorthodox style choices, perfectly embody the metrosexual spirit. In his writings, Simpson denounced the identity crisis of contemporary Western man, whose insecurity makes him easy prey for advertising promises. Despite this, in June 2003 the multinational advertising agency Euro RSCG (2003) published a report with research on new trends in male consumption, in which the term metrosexual was used to designate a profitable, rapidly growing market segment. The media - whether specialized in marketing and advertising, or directed towards final consumers - gave great prominence to the news, to the point that in 2003 the term "metrosexual" was voted the word of the year by the American Dialect Society due to its influence on U.S. media discourse. Manuals were even produced on how to be the perfect metrosexual, and various more or less serious online tests were developed to assist men in diagnosing to what extent they were metrosexuals. A pack of tarot cards and an episode of the cartoon *South Park* were dedicated to the metrosexual.

In the world of fashion, Italian designers were the first to ride the trend. In January 2013, at the men's fashion shows in Milan, the lead item in the Giorgio Armani collection was the Beckham jacket, conceived for the soccer player who, not coincidentally, became one of the designer's main endorsers. In June 2003 it was D&G's turn, as they had a model walk the runway in jeans and a red t-shirt with the word "David" on it, stressing that they had dressed both Beckham and his wife Victoria (the just as famous former Spice Girl) for a long time. In the subsequent months, many fashion, beauty and lifestyle companies launched products and services conceived more or less for the metrosexual man.

Source: drawn from Rinallo (2006).

To avoid the risk of "deviant" innovations, textile and clothing companies should therefore act to carefully analyze the evolution of consumer preferences and the products developed by numerous companies, in their own and related segments: an operation which is inconceivable for small companies with limited resources, though. The availability of shared trends is thus a formidable tool to understand the evolution of the relevant macro-environment and to reduce the intrinsic risk of the collection development process.

It is important to stress that the activity of predicting trends is not neutral with respect to the reality it aims to represent. To the extent that a trend identified by an authoritative source is able to influence the innovation choices of textile and clothing manufacturers, and subsequently, of consumers' purchases and usage, it takes on the character of a self-fulfilling prophecy.

2. The actors (i): trend producers and hunters

Contrary to the widespread idea that fashion trends are launched by the most famous brands and designers, in the textile and clothing world no company is an island, and trends that emerge at a given time are always the result of the interaction of numerous subjects that mutually influence each other and operate at various levels of the supply chain. Figure 1 shows the main actors and the relations of mutual influence among them.

Upstream of the process, textile and clothing companies, especially if they are small, are often accompanied in the collection development activities by companies whose business expressly consists of identifying and codifying fashion trends. The existence of trend hunters, often colorfully defined with the expression *cool hunter*, is well-known and not limited to the fashion world. The methods adopted by those persons have in fact been amply codified (for example, Proni, 2007; Vejlgaard, 2008). In the textile and clothing sector there are also specialized organizations, denominated *bureaux de style*, that deal with translating the consumption macro-trends emerging in society into concrete indications for the innovation of textile and clothing products (Guercini & Ranfagni, 2003). For example, to greatly simplify the terms of the problem and avoid an overly technical discussion, the heightened environmental awareness of consumers can be "translated" into the indication of preference for natural fibers,

Figure 1 The actors in the trend spreading process

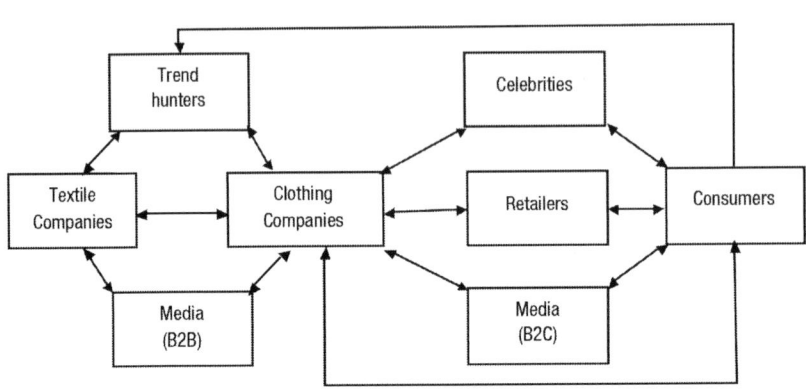

or even better organic fibers, with respect to synthetic fibers, and natural colorings rather than artificial ones. The *bureaux*, which are usually small, generally summarize their information in documents, known as *cahier de tendance*, with a strong visual impact.

The *producers of fibers, yarns and fabrics*, through their own semi-annual collections, provide important stimuli for innovation to apparel manufacturers. In addition to technical aspects able to enhance clothing performance (e.g. elastic, water-repellant, water-resistant, stain-resistant, anti-bacterial characteristics), the main decision-making areas regarding the development of textile collections include the fibers used (e.g. wool, cotton, linen, silk, acetate, lycra), the colors (red, coral, burgundy; hot summer colors, cold metallic colors; water colors), texture (irregular grains, structured weaves, light textures, satin, lace), finishings (fades, corrosion, dyeing, prints, layers) and patterns (flowery patterns, lines, ethnic decorations, Indian-style embroidery, Prince of Wales, pied-de-poule, etc.).

In this phase of the process the large specialty fairs in the sector, like *Première Vision* in Paris and *Milano Unica* in Milan (fabrics) and Pitti Filati in Florence (yarns for knitwear), serve as important platforms for the coordination of the collection development activities of many small companies (Golfetto & Mazursky, 2004; Rinallo & Golfetto, 2006 and 2011; Golfetto & Rinallo, 2008; Bathelt, Golfetto, & Rinallo, 2014). Given that new fabrics and yarns are presented six months prior to the collections of finished products, a visit to those events is a must for companies in the textile/clothing and related sectors (Guercini, 2003), as they can gain detailed knowledge of emerging trends in advance.

Box 2. Première Vision and the trend consultation mechanism

Première Vision was founded in 1973 as an entity for the joint promotion of a group of 15 textile companies in Lyon that, after a few years, began to meet before the exhibition to coordinate their product development activities through common guidelines. The trade show then opened to other producers, first from France and then from the rest of Europe, selected based on strict criteria regarding quality and innovation of collections, and began to make important investments for the trend concertation activity, leading it to become the most important event in the sector, with visitors from around the world. The term concertation, borrowed from political parlance, sheds light on how the activity of identifying and spreading trends is not the result of a technical analysis of the environment with a single point of arrival, but rather of decision processes carried out through negotiation from different viewpoints on different futures, all equally possible.
In the initial phase, trends are identified thanks to support from experts. To make that activity more effective, starting in 1997 *Première Vision* created an International Observatory that operates on a global scale to identify social-cultural trends able to impact the textile and clothing industry. The Observatory's analyses are conducted by a broad network of specialists that includes cool hunters and *bureaux de style*, but also architects, designers, experts in new technologies, sociologists and anthropologists. The trends identified are then validated in the context of consultation meetings that bring together representatives of the entire supply chain. At the concertation tables there are representatives of business associations in the textile sector and upstream, downstream and related industries, that interact until they reach a consensus.
Subsequently, the trends are communicated to the *Première Vision* exhibitors, months in advance of the trade show, through *ad hoc* seminars and various types of documentation (trend books, color palettes, CD-ROMs, etc.). The ideas underlying the trends are expressed with metaphors and evocative images. By way of example, one of the fabric trends for the 2010/2011 fall-winter season was summarized with the keyword "rudimentary" and described as follows: "From a world lying fallow, extracting unrefined elements, almost raw materials, to construct a soundly optimistic future. Fabrics with rough or industrial aspects, references to fundamental materials and to natural wear and tear, interpreted through the refinement of colors and handles" (*Première Vision*, 2009). The exhibitors use those guidelines to develop fabric collections that, despite being different, unavoidably have common elements and thus turn out to be very compatible with one another.
During the trade show, the trends have become reality. One the one hand, the samples presented to the buyers by the exhibitors reflect one trend or another. On the other hand,

Première Vision sets up trend areas with a strong visual impact, produced by artistic combinations of the fabrics. The visitors spend hours inside those areas, touching the fabrics, taking notes, having discussions and drawing inspiration for the development of their collections. Many do not intend do business with the exhibitors, and participate in *Première Vision* only because it is a special observatory for trends. This is true for textile companies that compete with the exhibitors and upstream companies in the sector (fibers, yarns, technologies, services) and related areas (leather, accessories). Thanks to coverage by specialized media, the trends produced at *Première Vision* also reach operators who have not participated in the event. As a consequence, many other textile producers, even in emerging countries with comparative cost advantages, develop collections inspired by those trends, thus contributing to their diffusion.

Source: drawn from Rinallo & Golfetto (2006).

Box 3. Dolce & Gabbana rosaries

It is known that the rosary is one of the most popular forms of prayer in the Catholic Church. Its use as a fashion accessory spread among consumers starting in the 1980s, thanks to the use made by the pop star Madonna in numerous concerts and videos such as *Like a Prayer*. More recently, the rosary has come back in style thanks to the designers Domenico Dolce and Stefano Gabbana. During their 2003 spring/summer fashion show, a rosary was worn by male models in swimsuits with chiseled bodies and by sensual female models who were wearing only black lace lingerie. The provocation hit the mark and the news spread around the world. D&G rosaries were then offered for sale, with prices up to hundreds of euros. Cheaper versions that were hard to distinguish from the D&G rosaries appeared immediately afterwards in the accessory departments of H&M and at street vendors. Rosaries were also worn in public by global celebrities (David Beckham, Britney Spears) and Italian personalities (Costantino Vitagliano), contributing to giving the trend visibility - adopted both spontaneously and as a result of the brand's celebrity relations. Negative reactions from religious authorities came quickly, but for fashion-oriented consumers the rosary rapidly became a must; the condemnation actually contributed to increasing its allure. For some, rosaries become a way to reconcile the sacred and the profane. Others consider it merely a fashion accessory, without any particular spiritual meaning, but able to attract eyes in situations such as the beach or a disco. As the trend gradually spread, even consumers who were initially skeptical about wearing a religious symbol on their neck in profane situations were enticed to try. After a couple of seasons, the rosary lost its novelty effect. Wearing one around the neck no longer made news, celebrities found other ways to attract attention, and consumers also got tired of it. The rosary is no longer a fashion item, and has returned to principally religious use.

Source: drawn from Rinallo *et al.*, (2012).

Among *apparel companies*, few are able to launch independent trends, that do not reflect what has been anticipated by cool hunters and incorporated into textile collections for a specific season. Recent research (Cappetta, Cillo & Ponti, 2006) has shed light on the fact that a limited number of "usual suspects" are the sources for the fashion trends spread by the most important fashion magazines. The companies are not necessarily the largest or those with the highest sales, such as giants like H&M or Zara, that rather than launching their own trends, tend to go with the flow.

On the other hand, companies with successful brands such as Armani, Prada and Dolce & Gabbana "set trends". In many cases, thanks to the considerable resources available to them, those companies are able to influence the content of editorials and obtain a level of coverage of their collection that is roughly proportional to the advertising investments at a single publication (Rinallo & Basuroy, 2009; Rinallo *et al.*, 2013). In addition, the stylistic leadership of those companies means that the innovations they propose are immediately picked up by competing companies around the world. Without going into the merits of the debate on copyright protection, we should stress that the phenomenon of imitation (and in extreme cases, counterfeiting), despite economically damaging innovative companies, is a necessary step without which it would be difficult for those innovations to take hold as trends among consumers.

3. The actors (ii): media, retailers and celebrities

As we have already argued, in the upstream phases of the supply chain, trends are constructed collectively through contributions from a broad number of actors who at times interact with each other in the context of relational platforms like those represented by large fairs, and that in other cases make independent decisions on the development of collections that are similar because they have originated from the same cultural stimuli. Despite this, the number of innovations that are launched on the market every six months is too high, and downstream of the process, other actors intervene that act to select a limited number of trends to submit to the attention of the general public. First among these is the media, whose editorial decisions provide visibility to certain trends, and not to others; and also retailers, whose assortment and visual merchandising choices give the consumer the concrete possibility to purchase the products. In a certain sense those subjects play the role of gatekeeper. That is, they periodically review an enormous volume of new products and potential trends, and with their choices (editorial and assortment, respectively), they give the trends visibility and favor/hinder their diffusion (McCracken, 1986; Hirsch, 1972).

Box 4 The Devil Wears Prada

In *The Devil Wears Prada*, one of the leading protagonists, Miranda Priesley (who is known to be the Hollywood version of Anna Wintour, the celebrated *editor-in-chief of Vogue America*), gives her own personal theory on how trends are born that put the media at the center of the process. In a memorable scene, the young intern Andy dares to laugh when Miranda and her collaborators try to match two almost identical belts with a dress for a photo shoot. Miranda scolds her:
"Oh. Okay. I see. You think this has nothing to do with you. You go to your closet and you select... I don't know... that lumpy blue sweater, for instance because you're trying to tell the world that you take yourself too seriously to care about what you put on your back. But what you don't know is that that sweater is not just blue, it's not turquoise. It's not lapis. It's actually cerulean. And you're also blithely unaware of the fact that in 2002, Oscar de la Renta did a collection of cerulean gowns. And then I think it was Yves Saint Laurent... wasn't it who showed cerulean military jackets? I think we need a jacket here. And then cerulean quickly showed up in the collections of eight different designers. And then it, uh, filtered down through the department stores and then trickled on down into some tragic Casual Corner where you, no doubt, fished it out of some clearance bin. However, that blue represents millions of dollars and countless jobs and it's sort of comical how you think that you've made a choice that exempts you from the fashion industry when, in fact, you're wearing the sweater that was selected for you by the people in this room from a pile of stuff".
With these words Miranda denies that consumers, even those who think they are not influenced by fashion, can make independent choices in terms of clothing. At the same time, between the lines she says that not even the large designers and brands are the ones who decide fashion trends. Certainly, Armani, Dolce e Gabbana and Oscar de la Renta can offer proposals, but Miranda the prima donna stresses that the large fashion magazines have a predominant role in selecting what become trends, influencing both the stylistic innovation choices of manufacturers and the purchase choices of consumers at the same time.

The field of fashion journalism is characterized by a concentration of influence in a limited number of publications and journalists who act as opinion leaders and *maître à penser*, so to say. In many sectors (such as wine, art, literature, film) there are critics able to influence the choices of resellers and consumers thanks to their independence and neutrality of judgment. In the field of fashion, on the other hand, there are very few voices considered to be truly critical (Davis, 1992). As regards written journalism, Suzy Menkes should be mentioned, who is considered as one of the most competent and "free" journalists in the world (including because the publication she writes for, the *International Herald Tribune*, does not accept advertisements from fashion companies). As regards magazines, it is mandatory to cite the various editions of *Vogue* around the world.

Retailers also act as gatekeepers. Many of the garments developed by apparel companies and presented on the runways and in showrooms are selected thanks to the purchase choices of independent distributors. It is not rare, in fact, for some of the garments presented not to be placed into production because they are not popular with retailers. If the media bring trends to the attention of consumers, it is only when the products resulting from the trends are available at stores that they can begin to spread on the market.

Celebrities, in addition to giving visibility to trends thanks to the accompanying media sensation, transfer the symbolic meanings they embody to the trends (McCracken, 1989). Consumption products and habits thus become trendy because they are adopted by celebrities who represent certain values and lifestyles. In this way, a trend acquires symbolic value and better lends itself to express the identity of consumers (or, at least, those target groups that see themselves in those celebrities). The cases discussed in Box 1 and 3 both refer to the role of celebrities such as Madonna or David Beckham as creators or spreaders of trends. Many large fashion companies, recognizing the trend-setting role played by VIPs, carry out *celebrity relation* activities in order to promote the spread of videos or photographs that show the personality in question wearing their products. Occasions such as Oscar Night thus become marathons for the most famous brands, that try to dress the highest number of candidates for the prestigious prize.

In that situation of mutual influence between multiple actors, consumers are at the beginning and end of the process of trend diffusion. They are at the end because, with their decisions, they have the last word on what will become a trend. And they are at the beginning because they hunt for trends and innovative companies pay a lot of attention to the way certain groups of consumers dress, whose style is thought to anticipate the stylistic development of society as a whole. Think of the gay community and ethnic communities (for example the African-American ghetto in the United States), professional communities (creative personnel at ad agencies, artists, professional athletes), and specific segments of consumers (surfers, snowboarders, motorcyclists, fashion enthusiasts), in which interesting consumption innovations are born. When the fashion industry adopts those styles, they lose their expressive value for the consumers who created them, who often then abandon them to create new, original trends. And thus the process starts again.

4. The geography of trends

Fashion trends originate in specific geographic locations. There are some (not many) centers in which trends originate, to then spread towards many peripheries. It is known that the first - and for some time the only - capital of fashion was Paris. The trends developed by the *couturier* in the French capital spread around the world thanks to the sale of models to local tailors who could thus satisfy requests from their clients to dress "in the latest Parisian fashion". After World War II a gradual increase of the number of cities aiming to be fashion capitals began. In the 50s, Florence earned a place in fashion geography thanks to the system of fashion shows conceived by G.B. Giorgini (Pinchera, 2009; Rinallo & Pinchera, 2013). Subsequently, it was Rome's turn, the city that had become Hollywood on the Tiber, through the association between stars and the tailors and fashion creators in the Italian capital. In the 60s, with the rebellion and impatience of the youth that extended to the way their parents dressed and the diktats of designers, new cities emerged with established youth cultures: London (known as swinging London) and New York. With the advent of prêt-à-porter, it was finally Milan's turn, thanks to the link between designers and the manufacturing industry.

The cities currently considered to be at the top of the fashion hierarchy due to their prestigious fashion weeks are Paris, Milan, New York and London. In the last ten to fifteen years though, there has been an exponential growth of the number of cities that organize fashion weeks to provide visibility to the stylistic innovations of local designers and brands. The trends that emerge from those cities rarely succeed in obtaining significant coverage from the international media, though. In addition, many cities, despite not having fashion weeks, are considered cultural epicenters due to the specific consumer culture that distinguishes them. The geography of fashion is thus much more fragmented than in the past, and truly global trends co-exist with more local trends, making the work of cool hunters more interesting.

5. Social media and the new role of consumers in spreading trends

The panorama as just described has changed profoundly since the start of the 2000s thanks to the spread of the web and social media, that have altered the influence mechanisms that traditionally governed the relationships between the key actors in the fashion world, giving consumers more power. Social media make word-of-mouth processes more visible, and extend consumers' opinion leadership from the personal network of family members, friends, co-workers and acquaintances, to a potentially global audience. Furthermore, opinions that were previously fleeting and remembered only by those who heard them now become permanent, as they are durably recorded in cyberspace and accessible for a long time after having been expressed. In terms of credibility, the opinions of consumers are often seen as more authentic (because they are not motivated by particular interests) and thus may be more persuasive with respect to those of traditional media (which are burdened by the suspicion of undue interference from advertisers). The phenomenon is widespread and does not regard only fashion: just think of the role taken on by consumer reviews in sectors such as film, hotels, restaurants and automobiles, and the emergence of virtual communities of consumers and professionals who, by discussing the merits and defects of products and services, have reduced the role of advertising. Consumers thus have a more active role than in the past, and can contribute to the emergence and success of trends much more directly than in the past.

Social media have also become a social field dominated by its own rules, where it is possible for some consumers to acquire a level of fame sufficient to transform the publication of contents into an actual business activity. In the terms shown in Figure 1, thanks to social media consumers can rise to the level of celebrities themselves and perform functions of creation/ spreading of fashion trends similar to that of traditional media. Bloggers like the Italian Chiara Ferragni with her *The Blonde Salad* (over 3 million followers on Instagram in 2015) or Aimee Song (the creator of *Song of Style*, with 1.9 million followers on Instagram and over 28,000 members of her Youtube channel in 2015) began their careers managing their own fashion blogs in which they published pictures of looks with combinations that expressed their own personal style. As their visibility grew, the bloggers began to draw the attention of the classic actors in the fashion world, becoming models, guests of honor at events, and designers of capsule collections, thus increasing the visibility of the respective brands thanks precisely to the number of their followers. No longer limited to the tool of the blog, now bloggers use all social media (Instagram, Flickr, Youtube, Twitter) and by doing so, multiply the scope of their influence.

Companies and traditional media initially resisted the social media revolution and the advent of these new actors who were outside of the regular dynamics in the sector. According to rumors, the aging fashion editors of the best-known fashion magazines turned up their nose when they found themselves sharing the front rows of fashion shows with bloggers who were barely beyond puberty. The organizers of fashion weeks also found it difficult to prepare the infrastructure necessary to update blogs in real time (Wi-Fi and the possibility to recharge devices). Today the most successful bloggers, with their millions of followers, are well integrated into the institutions of the fashion system. Fashion blogger has become a sought-after and envied profession, but it is important to remember that - like many other environments - social media is a competitive game where many fail and very few become stars. The classic actors (brands and media) become necessary to consecrate the bloggers who 'really count', rather than the wannabes, inviting them to their events, supplying them with their garments and accessories, etc. In addition, fashion houses increasingly hire bloggers for their digital PR initiatives, to give their products more visibility. Thus the conflict of interests that regards traditional media is now an issue in this area as well.

The empowerment of the consumer made possible by social media does not end with the emergence of bloggers as a new category of influencers of purchases and creators of trends. Even without becoming celebrities, nowadays consumers influence fashion houses and other actors in the fashion system in a way that may be less evident, but not less important. The actions of a large number of consumers on social media, who interact with each other in an uncoordinated way, exercise very strong forms of influence on key actors in the world of fashion and lead to the emergence of new trends in an even more unpredictable way than in the past. By posting pictures of their favorite outfits or notable styles they have seen on the street, consumers influence designers, stylists, journalists, photographers and *bureaux de style*, generating new aesthetics that impact the development of products and also the way these are communicated. Whereas bloggers initially imitated fashion professionals in their pictures, now the professionals themselves are increasingly finding inspiration in the fresh creativity of consumers (Dolbec & Fischer, 2015).

The world of social media can even provide an opportunity for more coordinated forms of collective action aimed at exercising pressure on the fashion world. The emblematic case is that of the pressure brought to bear on fashion houses by 'curvy' consumers, who by drawing inspiration from the fat acceptance movement, in some cases have succeeded in creating a critical mass of bloggers and celebrities and convinced some brands - who are notoriously reluctant to develop 'plus size' collections for fear of weakening the product's brand image - to take into account the needs of a neglected niche in the market (Scaraboto & Fischer, 2013).

The new centrality of consumers, and the greater visibility of their stylistic preferences thanks to social media, in a certain sense makes the work of trend hunters easier, as they can now search for emerging styles sitting comfortably in their homes in front of the computer, instead of observing them in the field or leafing through magazines. Thanks to social media, fashion companies can also obtain immediate feedback on their products, instead of going through focus groups, surveys and other traditional methods of market research. The digital revolution has thus in many ways made the trend affirmation process more fragmented, as the emergence of new technologies and social platforms has made trends themselves change continuously. Big data technology, which is expected to be able to predict the behavior of consumers starting with weak signals in the near future, will certainly impact the fashion world and the processes of prediction/affirmation of stylistic trends.

Bibliography

Bathelt, H., Golfetto, F., & Rinallo, D. (2014), *Trade Shows in the Globalizing Knowledge Economy*, Oxford University Press, Oxford (UK).

Cappetta, R., Cillo P., & Ponti, A. (2006), "Convergent designs in fine fashion: An evolutionary model for stylistic innovation", *Research Policy*, 35, pp. 1273-1290.

Davis, F. (1992), *Fashion Culture and Identity*. University of Chicago Press, Chicago.

Dolbec, P.-Y. & Fischer, E. (2015), "Re-fashioning a field? Connected consumers and institutional dynamics in markets", *Journal of Consumer Research*, 41 (6): 1447-1468.

Euro RSCG (2003), *The Future of Men*. Unpublished Research Report. New York, RSCG.

Golfetto, F. & Mazursky, D. (2004), "Competence-based marketing", *Harvard Business Review* (December), pp. 26-27.

Golfetto, F., Rinallo, D. (2008), "Reshaping markets through collective marketing strategies. Lessons from the textile industry". In K. Tollin & A. Carù (editor), *Strategic Market Creation: Realizing Radical Innovation from a Marketing Perspective*, Wiley, New York.

Guercini, S. (2003), *La Conoscenza di Mercato del Vertice d'Impresa*. Franco Angeli, Milan.

Guercini, S. & Ranfagni, S. (2003), "The role of bureau de style in the entrepreneurial network for textile product innovation", Proceedings of the 19th Conference of the *Industrial Marketing and Purchasing Group*, Lugano (Switzerland), 4-6 September.

Hirsch, P. (1972), "Processing fads and fashions: An organization-set analysis of cultural industry systems", *American Journal of Sociology*, 77(4), pp. 639-659.

Hirschman, E. (1986), "The creation of product symbolism", *Advances in Consumer Research*, 13, pp. 327-331.

McCracken, G. (1986), "Culture and consumption: A theoretical account of the structure and movement of the cultural meaning of consumer goods", *Journal of Consumer Research*, 13 (June), pp. 71-84.

McCracken, G. (1989), "Who is the celebrità endorser? Cultural foundations of the endorsement process", *Journal of Consumer Research*, 16 (3), pp. 310-321.

Pinchera, V. (2009), *La Moda in Toscana e in Italia: Dalle Origini alla Globalizzazione*, Marsilio, Venice.

Première Vision (2009), "A201011W fashion info", Press Kit, June.

Proni, G. (2007), *Leggere le Tendenze: Nuovi Percorsi di Ricerca per il Marketing*. Lupetti, Milan.

Rinallo, D. (2007), "Metro/Fashion/Tribes of men: Negotiating the boundaries of men's legitimate consumption". In B. Cova, R. Kozinets, A. Shankar (editors), *Consumer Tribes: Theory, Practice, and Prospects*. Elsevier/ Butterworth-Heinemann.

Rinallo, D. & Basuroy, S. (2009), "Does advertising influence media coverage of advertiser?", *Journal of Marketing* (November), pp. 33-46.

Rinallo, D., Basuroy, S, Wu, R., & Jeon, H.J. (2013) "The media and their advertisers: Exploring ethical dilemmas in product coverage decisions", *Journal of Business Ethics*, 114 (3), 425-441.

Rinallo, D., Borghini, S., Bamossy, G., & Kozinets, R.V. (2012), "When sacred objects go b®a(n)d: Fashion rosaries and the contemporary linkage of religion and commerciality". In D. Rinallo, P. Maclaran, L. Scott, (editors), *Consumption and Spirituality*, Routledge, London (UK).

Rinallo, D. & Golfetto, F. (2006), "Representing markets: The concertation of fashion trends by French and Italian fabric producers", *Industrial Marketing Management*, 35 (7): 856-869.

Rinallo, D. & Golfetto, F. (2011), "Exploring the knowledge strategies of temporary cluster organizers: A longitudinal study of the EU fabric industry trade shows (1986-2006)", *Economic Geography*, 87 (4), 453-476.

Rinallo, D., Golfetto, F., & Gibbert, M. (2006), "Consocia et impera: How the French and Italian fabric producers cooperate in order to affirm the dominant design in the fashion industry". In M. Gibbert & T. Durand (editors), *Strategic Networks*, Blackwell, Strategic Management Society Book Series, Oxford.

Rinallo, D. & Pinchera, V. (2013), "Exploring the link between nation branding and commercial mythmaking: The construction and reception of Italian fashion", paper presented to *Consumer Culture Theory Conference*, Tucson, Arizona (USA), 13-16 June.

Simpson, M. (1994), "Here come the mirror men", *The Independent*, 15 November.

Simpson, M. (2002), "Meet the Metrosexual", *Salon.com*, 22 July.

Scaraboto, D., Fischer, E. (2013), "Frustrated Fatsionistas: An institutional theory perspective on consumer quests for greater choice in mainstream markets", *Journal of Consumer Research*, 39 (Aprile), pp. 1234-1257.

Vejlgaard, H. (2008), *Trend: Capire oggi ciò che farà tendenza domani*. Etas, Milan.

5 Market Analysis and the Formulation of Guidelines

by *Giorgio Brandazza and Paola Varacca Capello*

1. The definition of collection guidelines

In Chapter 3 we mentioned how the formulation of guidelines is the starting point of the collection development process. In this phase the company must bring together a series of stimuli that come from sales data, client judgments and emerging trends, to rationally plan the new offer and give a precise direction to the subsequent phases (Brannon & Divita, 2015).

In the development of any collection there are two design areas: the aesthetic-stylistic area (where creativity is key) and the quantitative and structural area (where managerial skills prevail). Some experts call the first the *soft* part of the collection and the second the *hard* part. These areas derive from the choices of positioning and target, and thus from previous collections, unless a new collection/line is being developed. The positioning and target can already be consolidated, or have the need to evolve; in the latter case, defining guidelines that are different from the previous guidelines becomes a decisive factor.

Therefore, the collection guidelines follow two tracks (Varacca Capello, 1993): on the one hand there is the development of inputs for the style, which can be a more or less formal process; on the other, there is the definition of the elements of the collection structure, on which the merchandising plan (to which Chapter 6 is dedicated) will subsequently be constructed.

The aesthetic and innovative contents of the collection must be harmonized with the brand's stylistic identity and the seasonal trends. As regards those variables, there are often situations that can become critical if not managed in a balanced fashion:

- some companies invest significant economic and human resources in research activities that, despite not neglecting trends, aim to create strongly original elements in the collection, even at the risk of straying from the most popular emerging concepts. In those cases, the sources of "special" inspiration (historical company archives, artistic productions, vintage selections, etc.) become central as the origin of the creative process and as the dominant theme of the narrative that will then be constructed around the original ideas in the proposal; for example, Dolce & Gabbana dedicated its SS 2015 collection to the Spanish influence in Sicily between the 16th and 17th centuries;
- at times it is necessary to revise the brand's stylistic identity (or some of its elements), for various reasons, such as a desire to rejuvenate the target, or the adoption of new values. In these cases the role of the creative director is decisive. The case of Gucci is emblematic, when the entry of the designer Tom Ford and the development of *prêt-à-porter* introduced elements of sensuality and aggressiveness that until then had not been present in the experience of the brand, whose iconic elements were however revived. The new themes were translated into both product choices and very strong communications campaigns. Another example was the return of the trench coat and the repositioning of Burberry at the high-end of the market, implemented by the manager Angela Ahrendts and the designer Christopher Bailey. A more recent case is represented by the difficulties of the fashion retailer Abercrombie & Fitch (see Box 1).

From the standpoint of the quantity and structure of the collection, the definition of the guidelines consists of four main elements:

1. The definition of the *seasonal offer*, that is, a) in how many and what parts the collection will be structured, b) which targets, and c) what occasions of use, product categories and product types will be offered. Examples of questions to be answered before the design phase are: "will a division still exist between the pre-collection and the principal collection?", "will the fashion collection still be divided into three delivery packages?", "will we still deliver the

5 MARKET ANALYSIS AND THE FORMULATION OF GUIDELINES

Box 1. The revival of Abercrombie & Fitch

The American fashion retailer Abercrombie & Fitch, whose principal target is adolescents, experienced a long period of popularity and success until 2010, after which competition from its low-cost rivals and a gradual deterioration of the brand's image led to a drop in sales and the closing of numerous stores. This caused the departure of the CEO in 2014.
What changes does Abercrombie & Fitch need to make to its collections? According to an expert in the sector, there are various issues to be dealt with:
- the company must maintain its superiority in product quality over its lower level competitors, but without insisting on finishings and other details that young clients don't notice; prices could be decreased by 5-7.5% this way, to improve competitiveness;
- it must avoid following fashionable colors, especially those fluo colors that stray from its tradition;
- it must present a very broad and strong offer in the evergreen product categories, in particular sweaters, flannel shirts, Oxford shirts, t-shirts and skirts, that even without producing sales increases are important to define the brand's identity;
- the company needs to expand in accessory categories, like glasses, women's bags, travel bags, moccasins and leather jackets, that are close to the brand's lifestyle values and go well with existing categories;
- the women's collections can afford to follow trends more closely and propose prints and imaginative patterns (flowers, asymmetry, etc.);
- it is time to remove the logo from the product, or make it less evident, accepting the fact that it is no longer in fashion.

Source: Zanzi (2014), abridged from.

summer collection at the beginning of April?", "is a small basic/casual assortment appropriate to meet needs of comfort?", "and formalwear?", and "do we want to expand the proposal to target the men's market, neglected to this point?"

2. The management of the *complexity* judged acceptable for the season, given by the list and total number of SKUs. This indication, even if it must not be coercive, is the basis for an efficient management of the development process and the starting point to construct the merchandising plan.

3. An initial general indication of volumes and the mix for parts of the collection and product categories. The temporal placement of the plan in an early phase leads to a difficulty to obtain an initial

indication of the volumes, especially when the sales department is still dealing with the imminent sales campaign from the season prior to the one to be planned. Nevertheless, it is impossible to start the collection process without at least general information regarding volumes and the mix; therefore the marketing and sales function must lengthen its view to provide the necessary indications, also in relation to distribution policies. For example, the plan for opening new locations is crucial for the advance assessment of the volumes to be produced.

4. Finally, the company must set clear goals regarding the *gross margins* anticipated from the collection. Close monitoring of this indicator is decisive for the company's profits and the top management must make its expectations clear well in advance, to avoid a situation where the collection project creates cost restrictions on the product from the start, that will damage the margins of the collection. The gross margin also corresponds to the anticipated quality/price ratio; from this standpoint as well, it must be defined before the creative function launches the design phase.

In business practice, these elements are not always clearly distinguished, and the activities regarding the planning of the collection are variously divided between the figures involved, such as creative directors, brand managers, merchandisers and product directors.

In fashion jargon, guidelines are commonly called briefs, even though they can actually enter into more detail than a mere general layout of the process. In some companies two collection briefs are used, one on style and the other that, starting from more or less strict and detailed guidelines, leads to the definition of the merchandising plan.

The briefs are always based on the analysis and processing of the information and data available on past collections (Bubbio, Cacciamani, Rubello, & Solbiati, 2009). That analysis is the subject of the following paragraphs. In addition, companies draw on information from the competition. Almost everyone conducts analysis of the price of competitors' articles that are comparable to its own, every season and in various markets (cities and countries). That monitoring allows for verifying the company's positioning in price terms; it can be combined with a broad analysis of rival offers, with regard to occasions of use, types of products present, and the breadth and depth of the range. In recent years, fashion companies have reinforced their intelligence activities in part due to the possibilities offered by communication on the Internet and online sales (Rocamora, 2013). A precious source of information is also represented by suppliers (of fabrics, accessories, etc.) and by all operators in the supply chain in general.

2. Analysis of sales data

All companies analyze sales data, with a varying degree of detail, using it in a more or less strict way to formulate collection guidelines and devise the merchandising plan. As we will show later with concrete cases, the data itself is only relatively important, whereas the essential aspect is to properly and intelligently interpret that data, an activity that can be effectively developed if the different organizational functions are given the opportunity to discuss the results and validate the conclusions they reach. Data analysis not only supports the quantitative part of the collection plan, but if done well, can also provide ideas for style.

Companies mainly develop information on unitary volumes, turnover, price segments and margins earned, with reference to:

1. products (parts of collections and deliveries, occasions of use, product categories, models, fabric/color variants, SKUs);
2. channels/clients (DOS, multibrand, duty free, etc.);
3. markets (geographic areas and single countries).

We will avoid a more strictly commercial analysis here, dedicated to channels and markets, to concentrate on the implications of the structure of the offer, seeking to verify levels of cancellations during the sales campaign, and also the presence of problems of fragmented production, or the coherence between production strategy and quantities to be produced per model/fabric and SKU.

In general the sales data (in terms of volumes and value) are divided into:

- sell-in: sales to sales agents;
- sell-out: sales to final customers (available directly to companies that manage stores).

It is necessary to mention the concept of sell-through as well, used to different extents in companies, that refers to the percentage of units sold with respect to those received, or delivered by the company, in a certain interval of time. This figure allows for determining how many goods have been sold at full price, for example, considering the period between delivery to stores and the start of the discount season.

The collection of this data obviously takes place continuously, so as to provide input for the decision-making process, that cannot wait until the end of the season. The sell-in data is available at the end of the sales campaign, for companies that work with a *programmato* logic. In many cases the information referring to the first two-three weeks of sales allow for the launch of so-called "blind" fabric orders. The sales campaign data is also useful to draw up the merchandising plan for the next corresponding collection. For example, the sell-in for SS 2014 will be available in October/November 2013, and thus can be used for SS 2015, conceived starting in January 2014.

The sell-out data is available through the course of the entire season. It is always necessary to distinguish between sales made at full price, and those at discounted prices. It is important to remember that the prices/revenue for the company change depending on whether it sells in its own stores (retail prices) or through agents (wholesale prices). One consequence is that overall turnover of companies that operate with diversified channels is a deceptive figure, since it sums sell-out data from its own stores with sell-in data to other channels.

Information can also be gathered on the process, relating to both development (evaluating how many articles were presented in the sales campaign, which actually sold, how many were added later), and to logistical/production aspects (articles ordered, delivered, etc.). The information on delivered goods can refer to both orders collected in the sales campaign and to those obtained subsequently as reassortments.

In the case of companies that produce materials (yarns, fabrics) there is an additional step: the collection presented undergoes an initial screening linked to the articles for which samples are actually requested. The collection of orders proceeds with these articles in a phase after the production of the samples.

Figure 1 lists some of the analyses that can be carried out to identify possible solutions, including possible results and causes. SKUs are used because the analyses must go into as much detail as possible, but the same reasoning can be applied for all intermediate dimensions of the collection.

5 Market Analysis and the Formulation of Guidelines

Figure 1 Analysis of collection data

Comparison between	Results and analysis
SKUs planned SKUs presented	The relationship between SKUs planned (defined in the plan) and SKUs actually presented, offers an initial verification of the efficacy and discipline of the company's merchandising process. If there is a significant deviation between what was planned and what was proposed, it is necessary to understand why (for example if the sales force requested numerous variants that led to an explosion of the codes for the season). In this sense, it is necessary to evaluate the consistency of these entries with respect to the themes chosen for the season. Additional analysis (relating to the sell-in) verifies the effectiveness of these decisions.
SKUs presented SKUs sold-in	When there are numerous cancellations of articles that have not been purchased, there is a problem of excess variety of the offer, that must be carefully studied. For example: is there is a concentration of cancellations in some areas of the offer such as specific price segments or specific offer areas? Let us suppose that cancellations are concentrated in high price segments, or in "release No. 3", or in the 'basic' collection. In this case, in order to develop the plan, it will be necessary to evaluate the efficacy of the price positioning defined, or the usefulness of "release No. 3" with a certain delivery timeframe, or the efficacy of a basic offer concentrated in an ad hoc collection. Other important and more detailed indications can come from analysis such as: the number of models cancelled compared to total models, the number of colors actually sold per model/fabric compared to those presented, etc. These additional analyses suggest other important detailed planning elements such as: the depth of color offers, the mix between basic colors and fashion colors, and other aspects as well.
SKUs sold-in SKUs delivered	When the level of deliveries is low compared to orders, there is a problem regarding service. It becomes necessary to identify what obstacles arose, if the cancellations were the consequence of too small orders, lack of delivery of fabrics or production problems. This figure can be updated between the first release in the plan, that is calculated when seasonal deliveries have just started, and its definitive version, that is published at the moment the deliveries have practically been completed. This figure refers specifically to the purchase and production area and is directly linked to the analysis presented in the subsequent point. In addition, it is necessary to evaluate the performance of the offer from a strictly productive standpoint through the analysis of parameters such as: a) the average pieces produced per model, per model/fabric, and per SKU (model/fabric/color), and also b) the concentration curve of the pieces produced (again per model, model/fabric, etc.). Those parameters are indicative of complexity of production and the consistency between the production choices made by the company and the distribution of actual volumes to be produced.
SKUs delivered SKUs sold-out	If the sell-out is low, there will be an inventory problem. The causes for this result need to be examined, for example by checking the actual delivery times, considering unforeseen weather events, problems of wearability or other aspects. The feedback from store managers, who gather input from final customers, is crucial.

Lastly, it is advisable to submit the quantitative assessments of offer performance to the sales function, to add client comments. The client is, by definition, an important source of information; in addition to comments on the contents of the offer, it is useful to collect those on its breadth and structure. For example, clients often request collections that are more distributed over the sales season, and more concentrated in terms of structure, that makes it easier to clearly identify them and formulate the purchases.

A crucial role in gathering information for companies that earn significant portions of their turnover with multibrand stores, is played by the agent. Thanks to the recent information technologies developed, agents now carry out the process of order collection and sales in general in a more precise and timely manner. If properly trained and involved, agents can be essential in constructing a valid collaborative relationship between producers and clients.

The analysis presented in Figure 1 refers to companies that distribute through independent stores, and thus carry out a sales campaign; for these companies it is very difficult to obtain sell-out data quickly, outside of general indications. The opposite is true for fashion retailers and for all producers who distribute exclusively or principally with their own stores: here the analysis concentrates on deliveries to stores and sell-out data. The immediate availability of information from the end market is one of the typical advantages of direct distribution, especially for offers with greater fashion content, where the ability to react rapidly to the choices expressed by customers is a weapon that allows for constructing competitive advantages. Companies that make use of both channels - direct and indirect - can benefit from integrating the analyses conducted for one with those obtained for the second, after properly considering their different aspects.

A broad variety of additional studies can be carried out based on collection types. As an example, we present an examination of price segments, to evaluate the consistency of the proposal with market needs, indicated by the sales results obtained in different segments. Figure 2 compares the FW 2012-2013 edition with the 2013-2014 edition of a knitwear collection, structured around three price segments: a core, or principal segment, and two positions in lower and higher segments, respectively. The table quantifies the percentage of sales obtained by each segment in the two years (in terms of SKUs). 2013-2014 shows a shift towards the high-end,

Figure 2 Analysis of FW retail collection sales prices

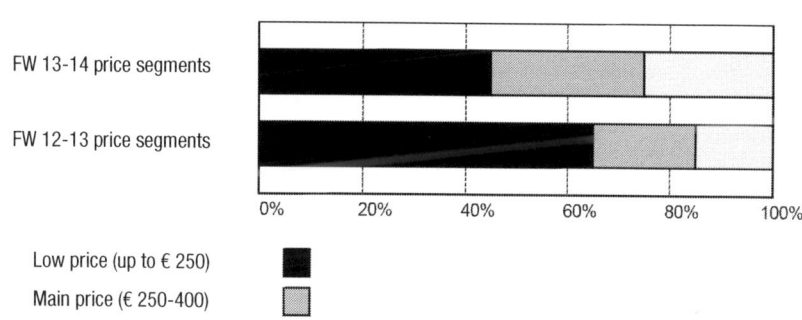

that covers approximately 25% of the SKUs, while the previous year was lower, at 20%. The portion of sales of SKUs in the lower segment also increased. As a consequence, the portion of low-price SKUs dropped from approximately 65% the first year to approximately 45% the second. This change in sales is in theory positive for the company, that can see its margins grow; but we must note that the figure for overall sales is lacking here, so it is possible that the distribution observed in 2013-2014 merely reflects a drop in sales of the low-price SKUs, without an increase in the absolute values of the other SKUs.

Only by comparing the price structure (that reflects the desired positioning of the collection) with the quantities sold during the season, can we evaluate the consistency of the proposal with the needs of the market. The analysis of which price segments saw better sales results also allows for verifying the success of the brand policy: if sales are concentrated in low-price areas, the brand probably has a positioning that is lower than desired.

3. ABC analysis

ABC analysis is one of the most useful and widespread instruments used to study sales distribution (or other quantities) with respect to categories of interest. This analysis is based on Pareto's law, which states that in any sum of factors to be examined, we can generally discover a small number of factors that have considerable influence on the effects; to the contrary, the remaining majority of factors have a small influence (Ishikawa, 1976). The most common application of ABC analysis is in warehouse management, where the different impact of the more and less critical articles is particularly evident. The name ABC comes from the practice of dividing the factors to be managed into three groups (A, B, C), calculating their respective effects.

In reading the sales data, ABC analysis requires identifying the elements that identify the collection (themes, models, fabrics, prices, etc.) and evaluating their impact on results, that can be the volumes, turnover or margins. In ABC analysis the units of analysis (articles, for example) will be ordered based on the result (sales volumes, for example) starting from the one with the best result and moving towards the one with the worst result. The first units are the bestsellers; the portions of sales they generate reflect their respective weight.

The example in Figure 3 illustrates an ABC analysis on ten small leather goods articles. The table on the left calculates the turnover for each article and its percentage weight on the collection's total sales. The second table orders the articles by decreasing weight on sales, and adds a column with the cumulative weight of the articles. These table is then translated into its graphic representation.

We note that the turnover for the first two articles (2 and 7) generates almost 80% of sales; this group is Class A. The next two articles, identified as Class B, provide an additional contribution of less than 10%. The last articles, Class C, make up approximately 10% of turnover. ABC analysis thus shows the possibility to reduce the complexity of the collection, planning a smaller number of articles to obtain a more focused offer. The cost savings (in collection development, production, inventory management, administration) can make up for the loss of revenues due to the fact that some customers could be disappointed by the more limited offer remaining.

5   MARKET ANALYSIS AND THE FORMULATION OF GUIDELINES   101

Figure 3   An example of ABC analysis

	Price	Volumes sold	Turnover (price x volume)	% of total turnover		% of total turnover	% of total turnover cumulative	Class
Article 1	€ 70	160	€ 10,500	4.5%	Article 2	42.3%	42.3%	A
Article 2	€ 105	950	€ 99,750	42.3%	Article 7	37.3%	79.6%	A
Article 3	€ 25	500	€ 12,500	5.3%	Article 3	5.3%	84.9%	B
Article 4	€ 65	60	€ 3,900	1.7%	Article 1	4.5%	89.4%	B
Article 5	€ 25	300	€ 7,500	3.2%	Article 5	3.2%	92.6%	C
Article 6	€ 10	520	€ 5,200	2.2%	Article 6	2.2%	94.8%	C
Article 7	€ 80	1,100	€ 88,000	37.3%	Article 10	1.8%	96.5%	C
Article 8	€ 46	60	€ 2,760	1.2%	Article 4	1.7%	98.2%	C
Article 9	€ 25	60	€ 1,500	0.6%	Article 8	1.2%	99.4%	C
Article 10	€ 60	70	€ 4,200	1.8%	Article 9	0.6%	100%	C

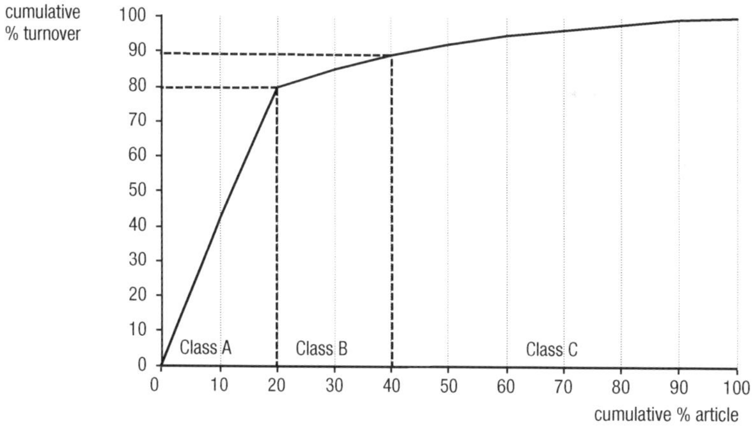

4. Some examples of data analysis and processing and definition of guidelines

4.1   *Variety in terms of models*

The following table (Figure 4a) shows the number of models per type of garment in a high-end women's collection for the FW season, with the respective sell-in data. The first column shows the number of models by type

Figure 4a Sell-in of a FW women's collection

Type of garment	Models	Pieces sold	Models/total models	Pieces sold/ total sales	Average pieces sold per model
suits	67	2,936	16%	9%	43.8
shirts	23	1,805	5%	6%	78.5
jackets	41	2,737	10%	8%	66.8
skirts	18	2,696	4%	8%	149.8
jerseys	9	796	2%	2%	88.4
knitwear	104	7,946	25%	24%	76.4
pants	17	4,547	4%	14%	267.5
leather	51	1,899	12%	6%	37.2
windbreakers	38	7,326	9%	22%	192.8
unsold models	53	0	13%	0%	0.0
Total collection	421	32,688	100%	100%	77.6

of garment. The second lists the number of pieces sold, again by type of garment. In the third column the number of models per type of garment is considered as a percentage of the total of the models in the collection (421); in the fourth column, the pieces sold per type of garment are presented as a percentage of the total of the pieces sold in the collection (32,688).

A comparison between the third and fourth columns allows us to see if the planning efforts on the variety of models have been adequately rewarded in terms of sales. Some items, in particular pants, skirts and windbreakers, sold well (14%, 8% and 22% of pieces, respectively) with a limited number of models (4% of the models proposed for pants and skirts, 9% for windbreakers). Other categories, such as suits and leather, had opposite results: despite considerable creative efforts (16% and 12% of the models created, respectively), the sales results were lower (9% and 6%). Knitwear shows a balanced situation between the models proposed (25%) and the pieces sold (24%).

In the last column, the number of pieces sold per type of garment is divided by number of models, obtaining an indicator of efficiency. In fact, the lower the number of pieces sold per model, the lower the reward for the planning effort dedicated to each model: some product areas (suits and leather) have very low averages and require a rethinking of the collection structure. Furthermore, this indicator allows for comparing which models sold a number of pieces higher or lower than the average, for each type of garment.

5   MARKET ANALYSIS AND THE FORMULATION OF GUIDELINES

Figure 4b   ABC analysis of sell-in data of collection

Type of garment	Models	Pieces sold	First 50% of sales	First 80% of sales	First 90% of sales	Last 10% of sales	100% of sales
suits	67	2,936	15%	33%	45	55	100%
shirts	23	1,805	13%	31%	44	56	100%
jackets	41	2,737	12%	35%	49	51	100%
skirts	18	2,696	9%	27%	36	64	100%
jerseys	9	796	23%	38%	46	54	100%
knitwear	104	7,946	13%	34%	46	54	100%
pants	17	4,547	11%	33%	44	56	100%
leather	51	1,899	13%	33%	47	53	100%
windbreakers	38	7,326	16%	37%	53	47	100%
unsold models	53	0	0%	0%	0	0	100%
Total collection	421	32,688	10%	28%	41%	59%	100%

In Figure 4b the sell-in data for the same collection is subjected to an ABC analysis to examine the excessive fragmentation that has already emerged. The models and pieces sold are the same as in the previous table. The new columns indicate the percentage of models that produced the first 50%, the first 80%, the first 90% and the last 10% of sales, for each type of garment. The values are presented in decreasing order of the models in terms of contribution to sales. For example, 50% of the suits sold were produced by 15% of the models (10), 80% from 33% of the models (22), and so on. What stands out is the strong concentration of sales of skirts, for which 9% of the models were responsible for 50% of sales; the types of garments with the best distribution of sales were jerseys, windbreakers, and suits.

Figure 4c represents the cumulative sales for the collection as a whole, and for the sale of jerseys. The softer curve of jerseys indicates that more models achieve significant sales than in the average of the collection. The curve for the collection is steep in absolute terms, demonstrating that many models have had limited sales results. This seems to indicate an excessive variety of the collection, that should be reduced in subsequent seasons.

It is nevertheless clear that numbers by themselves don't allow for reaching definitive conclusions. The company could have a tradition of strong creativity and be recognized and appreciated by the market for this ability. Therefore, even if it is advisable to reflect on limiting the number of models, it is primarily necessary to examine those which had poor results and

Figure 4c Cumulative curve for total collection and jerseys

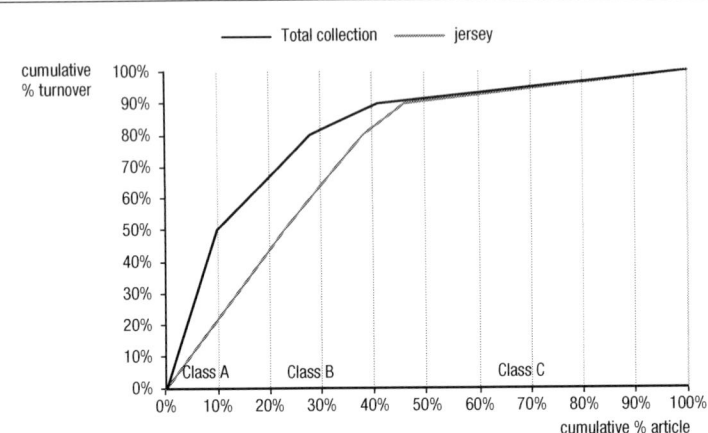

the reasons for that performance. For example, if certain designs or materials were not popular with the public, the recommendation to reduce the number of models becomes less convincing, or it can be postponed until after modifying or substituting the weak models.

4.2   *Positioning and variety*

The following example starts with the final sales data (sell-in) for a high-end licensed women's and men's collection, with a casual character, introduced to offer this function of use alongside the main line, and distributed in the same stores as the former. The tables in Figure 5a show the models in the women's collection divided by type of garment (clothing) and product categories (accessories), the models sold, the SKUs presented, the SKUs added in season and the SKUs cancelled. The SKUs sold have been obtained by summing the SKUs presented and added and subtracting those eliminated. The last columns show the pieces sold and the weight of the type of garment/category on the total of sold units.

The data allows us to reach an initial conclusion concerning the breadth of the offer: given that this is a complementary collection, the total look proposed may be excessive. That consideration is reinforced when we consider the sales results: if we observe the column of sold items we recognize that some products had a miserable performance. In clothing, jeans, t-shirts and knitwear represent 77.6% of sales. In accessories, belts, scarves and shoes cover 80.6%.

5   MARKET ANALYSIS AND THE FORMULATION OF GUIDELINES

Figure 5a   Sell-in data for FW women's collection

Clothing

Type of garment	models presented	models sold	SKUs presented	SKUs added	SKUs cancelled	SKUs sold	pieces sold	% pieces sold on total
jeans	23	16	138	33	68	103	133,805	39.3%
pants	22	16	35	1	9	27	23,887	7.0%
separates	9	4	11	0	7	4	919	0.3%
skirts	35	27	42	0	11	31	10,219	3.0%
suits	33	27	42	1	8	35	9,722	2.9%
jackets	16	12	22	4	8	18	2,388	0.7%
shirts	14	11	23	4	10	17	12,304	3.6%
t-shirts	56	53	72	2	9	65	92,167	27.1%
knits	53	51	53	5	9	49	38,281	11.2%
coats	26	23	55	3	31	27	14,384	4.2%
underwear	7	6	7	0	1	6	2,253	0.7%
Total collection	294	246	500	53	171	382	340,330	100%

Accessoires

Category	models presented	models sold	SKUs presented	SKUs added	SKUs cancelled	SKUs sold	pieces sold	% pieces sold on total
shoes	27	17	41	0	20	21	3,051	12.9%
bags and beauty cases	19	15	22	0	6	16	2,038	8.6%
small leather goods	1	1	1	0	0	1	197	0.8%
belts	21	16	23	0	4	19	12,070	51.2%
hats	10	0	10	0	10	0	0	0.0%
gloves	9	5	9	0	4	5	1,304	5.5%
scarves	15	10	15	0	5	10	3,904	16.5%
foulards	2	2	2	0	1	1	1,030	4.4%
Total collection	104	66	123	0	50	73	23,594	100%

The calculations presented in Figure 5b allow for more precise reflections on the women's clothing collection. The first column shows the SKUs presented, the second weighs these SKUs on the total of the collection, demonstrating that the best-selling kinds of items do indeed have a higher

Figure 5b   Elaborations of sell-in data for FW women's collection

Clothing

Type of garment	SKUs pre-sented	SKUs pre-sented/ total	SKUs can-celled	SKUs can-celled/ presented	Pieces sold	Pieces sold on SKUS sold	Pieces sold on SKUS sold	Models sold	Average pieces sold per model
jeans	138	28%	68	49%	133,805	103	1,299	16	8,363
pants	35	7%	9	26%	23,887	27	885	16	1,493
separates	11	2%	7	64%	919	4	230	4	230
skirts	42	8%	11	26%	10,219	31	330	27	378
suits	42	8%	8	19%	9,722	35	278	27	360
jackets	22	4%	8	36%	2,388	18	133	12	199
shirts	23	5%	10	43%	12,304	17	724	11	1,119
t-shirts	72	14%	9	13%	92,167	65	1,418	53	1,739
knits	53	11%	9	17%	38,282	49	781	51	751
coats	55	11%	31	56%	14,384	27	533	23	625
underwear	7	1%	1	14%	2,253	6	376	6	376
Total collection	500	100	171	34%	340,330	382	891	246	1,383

number of SKUs, although lower (52.6%) than their weight on units sold. This suggests that the SKUs of this type of item could be enriched, given the positive response in terms of sales. For shirts, suits, jackets and coats, the opposite is true, given that their weight on the SKUs shows a considerable creative effort associated with very low sales.

The third column looks at the SKUs cancelled, while the fourth calculates their proportion on those presented. The weight of the cancellations is really high for some categories: separates, jackets, shirts and coats and even jeans, for which the figure indicates the need to reconsider the idea of expanding the SKUs.

The first and sixth columns show the data on pieces and SKUs sold; the subsequent column derives the pieces sold per SKU. The result shows that too many types of items are below average, with particularly low data for separates and jackets. Similar conclusions can be drawn from the last two columns, which show the models sold and calculate the average sales per model.

Figure 6 performs calculations on the sell-in information for the men's collection, regarding the jeans category, for which the offer is divided into three price segments. The first column shows the SKU numbers for each

Figure 6 Examination of sell-in data for FW men's collection

Men's jeans

Price segment	SKUs	% SKUs	% of total sales (in value)
Low	50	34%	23%
Medium	64	44%	31%
High	29	20%	46%
Total	143	100%	100%

price segment, the second the percentages of the SKUs for each price segment with respect to the total SKUs of jeans, the third provides the percentages of turnover of jeans for each price segment. First of all, we can see that many SKUS (78%) are in the low and medium segments: this is not consistent with the collection's positioning, that is complementary to the top line also for menswear. It is not clear why creative effort should be concentrated in these segments, or why there should be excessive variety. It also emerges that the more costly jeans sell well (46% of total sales, although information on the prices is needed); this means that the company should enrich the offer in that price segment, to the detriment of others.

To summarize, even without the general picture of the collection, and calculating only some information on the sell-in, we can deduce that the licensee should seek to reduce the offer both in terms of product categories and number of variants proposed; on the other hand, a certain amount of attention should be paid to defining the price segments on which to focus.

4.3 *A different approach to seasonal collections*

In the examples above we have discussed the simplified case of a single seasonal collection, that by now does not reflect the characteristic temporal distribution of many fashion companies, as indicated in the previous chapters. The presence of multiple collections during one season complicates the problems (but also the opportunities) in analyzing the results. The variety of the SKUs, in particular, can be distributed over multiple collections, with certain functions of use that prevail in one, rather than in another.

Figure 7 Occasions of use and SKUs

Mix lifestyle collection: SS

Categories	Dressy / Cocktail special occasion	Easy / Cocktail	Basic item & Rich basic cross-season	Premium daywear	Leisure / Urban weekend	Total
Knitwear	5%	25%	20%	35%	15%	100%
Ready to wear	5%	25%	20%	35%	15%	100%
Leather			20%	40%	40%	100%

Percentage of SKUs with respect to total per category

FW and SS seasonal collections

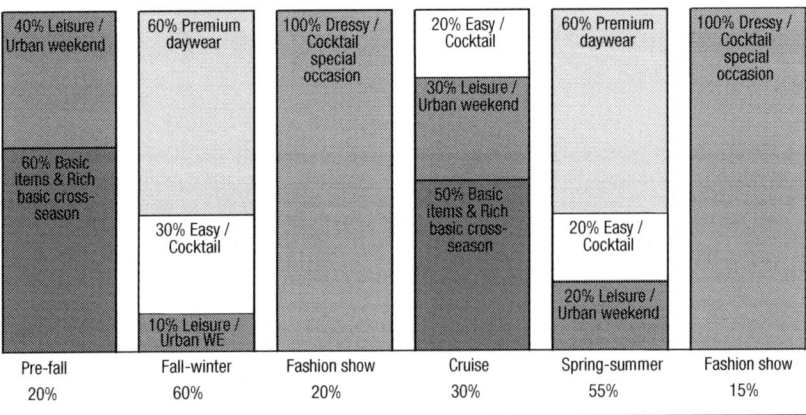

Percentages of SKUs with respect to total of the collection (in the boxes) and the season (in the lines)

Again as an example, Figure 7 presents the division of the clothing collections of a luxury company, divided by occasions of use and marked by multiple launches during the season. The first figure presents the SS offer in detail, that is spread over three product areas (knitwear, fabric and leather) and is divided into five occasions of use. The percentages indicate the numerical weight of the SKUs on each occasion of use with respect to the total product area. As can be seen, in clothing the categories Easy − Cocktail and Premium daywear absorb 60% of the SKUs; nevertheless, the interseasonal package Basic items & Rich items is robust and has the goal of maintaining a broad offer in stores also during the weeks at the end of seasons.

The second figure, that omits the divisions by product areas, presents the succession of the collections along the FW and SS seasons. The pre-season collections have two deliveries each, the principal ones have four each, while those for fashion shows do not involve deliveries. The consequences of greater variety of the SKUs for the principal collections can be seen here, even though their weight varies over the year for the occasions of use that characterize the offer.

Bibliography

Brannon, E. & Divita, L. (2015), *Fashion Forecasting*. Bloomsbury, London.
Bubbio, A., Cacciamani, A., Rubello, U., & Solbiati, M. (2009), *Il controllo di gestione nelle imprese del fashion*. IPSOA, Milan.
Ishikawa, K. (1976), "Guide to Quality Control", Asian Productivity Organization, Unipub.
Rocamora, A. (2013), "New fashion times: Fashion and digital media", *The Handbook of Fashion Studies*, pp. 61-77.
Varacca Capello, P. (1993), "Lo sviluppo delle collezioni nel sistema moda. Logiche e strumenti operativi", *Economia & Management*, 6, pp. 86-97.
Zanzi, C. (2014), "La dieta di Abercrombie", *Pambianco Magazine*, February 19, pp. 55-58.

6 The Balance between Creativity and Rationality in Collection Development: the Merchandising Plan

by *Giorgio Brandazza and Paola Varacca Capello*

1. The merchandising plan: content and methodology

The merchandising plan is the main tool used to fine-tune the product range. Below its main features are listed.
Before going into the details of its formulation, it should be noted that the preparation of the plan requires:

- a critical reading of the past,
- the formulation of development options for the product range,
- the setting of cost and price parameters of the product.

It is therefore a task in which the management team, guided by a rigorous analysis of performance and the identification of functional constraints, can define and formalize the seasonal product range. Strategy is thus translated into actions, choices, numbers, costs, suppliers and clients.

1.2 *When it is prepared*

The merchandising plan should be prepared and approved before beginning the design and development of the product. Its exact timing is determined by the specific cycles of presentation, sale and delivery of the planned collections. In companies that operate on a traditional seasonal cycle, the merchandising plan is prepared respectively in the month of December for the spring-summer collections (for sell-in in June-July of the following year and delivery to clients starting in December-January) and in June for the autumn-winter collections.
Such early timing suggests two important characteristics of the meth-

od: (a) first, the need for the merchandising plan to be unique, regardless of the number of seasonal collections; (b) second, the need to update the plan during the product development cycle.

In relation to the first factor, it must be emphasized that the plan should embrace the brand's entire offer during the entire seasonal cycle so that it can effectively guide and regulate the product range. It goes without saying that if the product range launches a "spring" collection and a "summer" collection with separate timings of sell-in and delivery, the plan should contemplate both phases and then be updated and revised when planning starts for the second phase; nevertheless the guidelines for the entire season should already be precisely stated in the first release of the document.

The update is a necessity imposed by the fact that, at the beginning of the season's product development cycle, the company receives information on both the "off"-season sell-out, (in the planning cycle of a spring-summer season that begins in December, in-store sales of the previous spring's collection begin in January and February, and their sell-out information is extremely important) as well as on the sell-in (the autumn-winter sell-in campaign begins in January in the same seasonal cycle). From an operational point of view it will be crucial to define a time limit for updates to the plan, in order to incorporate as much information as possible without letting the updates cause delays. In practice, therefore, the plan has an initial version and an updated version that incorporates changes and adjustments made necessary by ongoing operations.

1.2 *Who prepares it and who approves it*

A growing number of companies have created the position of merchandiser, although he/she does not always (hardly ever, we should say) perform the same duties in each company.

In the absence of the well-defined job position of "merchandiser" (which is described in detail below) the merchandising plan is prepared in the product development area with the cooperation of marketing, sales and production.

Proper merchandising requires in any case the full involvement of all first-line organizational functions and the formal approval of top management, whether represented by the General Manager or by the Business Unit manager (in practice, approval is given by those responsible for profitability). The involvement of the entire first line of management is crucial to the success of the process since the plan represents the link between the declaration of brand strategy and its operational realization.

1.3 The inputs for the construction of the merchandising plan and its contents

The merchandising plan is the guide for a proper development of the offer. Therefore, it must contain a series of precise quantitative and qualitative indications. As described below, the merchandiser is not a figure with strong decision-making power. The figure must develop plans (to be submitted for approval by the top management) with the assistance of all of the functions and based on precise management inputs (collection guidelines, dealt with in chapter 5). Below we again look at the four indispensible input elements for valid process management, that are based on a rigorous analysis of collection performance.

First of all, the company must clarify its market offer strategy, and therefore must define the collection structure for the season it is planning, being able to define the *overall number of SKUs* for the season.

A forecast of the collection structure cannot be developed without a first indication of *volumes* and *mix* per collection and product category. Lastly, the company must provide precise indications regarding the expected *gross collection profit*. The gross margin essentially indicates the anticipated price/quality ratio; as such, it must be defined before the creative function is launched in the planning phase.

Starting with these inputs, the plan must include the distribution of the SKUs over the components of the offer. The company must have a clear idea of the hierarchy of its offer and the variables of which it consists. The hierarchy defines various levels of aggregation of the articles based on the position of the brand on the market, for example:

- collections (basic and fashion collections);
- method of structuring the collection (in delivery packages, or in "themes or color stories", or outfits, or also in occasions of use);
- product categories (jackets, suits, knitwear, etc.), that in turn are divided by price segments (entry level, core, and high-end).

Secondly, the merchandising plan must contain the detailed structuring of the ratio between industrial cost, wholesale price and price to the public so as to offer precise indications on the product cost, the cost of raw materials (leather, fabrics and other items), and of cost range for manufacturing that are decisive for the industrial cost (think of the more or less industrialized work on a men's outerwear garment or the cost of washing in the jeans sector).

The method of reconstructing the ratio between industrial cost and product price varies greatly as a function of the type of company (direct production, use of external *façon* or pure marketing of products supplied by third party suppliers) and its degree of internationality in terms of production and distribution. The plan must therefore reconstruct in detail the relationship between the components of the industrial cost (raw materials, manufacturing, finishing) and the price to the public: an indispensable element for the planning of a profitable offer.

A good plan consists of numbers, in general and in detail, but numbers involve assumptions that need to be summarized in qualitative terms. In order to adequately study the question, it is always useful to recall the assumptions used for specific decisions; in this regard, we suggest compiling the figures as an element of company learning, in an enclosure or a strictly qualitative introduction, that remains as an important contribution to the company's knowledge and assets.

1.4   Who uses the merchandising plan

The merchandising plan's "natural" user is the design team. For the creative department, it becomes the reference grid, the actual canvas on which the collection is developed.

However, the plan is extremely important for other divisions both inside and outside the company. Within the company, the plan is used by the entire management team. Management has contributed to its development and established standards relating to each specific area of its responsibility (consider the cost/price relationship, where the production division determines the cost standards, just as the sales division commits to sales volumes and the marketing division determines price positioning and the distribution mark-up structure); the whole team is confronted with an organic document that summarizes specific divisional tasks as well as expected seasonal performance levels. In this sense, the natural consequence of the plan is the seasonal budget.

In the outside world, an important user of the plan is the licensed partner, who finds the licensor's requirements for the collection summarized in this document. Without detracting from the creative effort that each licensee must make, the merchandising plan summarizes the desired structure of the product range and, as such, enhances the dialogue between the two sides during product development.

2. The process and the main problems in building the plan

The merchandising process has certain important steps and methods which must be fully understood. In particular, we will concentrate on three main aspects:

1. the number and distribution of SKUs,
2. balancing the SKUs per price range,
3. the relationship between retail price and manufacturing cost of the product.

Experience suggests that these are the three most delicate steps of the process, which the company must carefully consider and plan.

2.1 *The number and distribution of the SKUs*

The first important issue in merchandising is the definition of the total number of SKUs in the collection and their distribution into the various sections of the product range. The number of SKUs is the first limit to be placed on the creative process since it immediately determines the level of complexity the company can sustain.

From a methodological point of view it is necessary to:

1. Precisely define the company's product hierarchy. In the case of collections of young adult sportswear we can find for example merchandise divided into men's and women's, both divided into a basic collection and a fashion collection, with the fashion collections divided into "launches" with predefined deliveries. In other cases, the collection may be broken down by color theme or "look". There is no attempt here to make an all-inclusive list, but rather to emphasize the need for a hierarchical approach to the product structure and its sustainable complexity.
2. Always operate within this hierarchy using a top-down logic in order not to risk discussing the number of SKUs in knitwear

launch number 3, before the following have been defined, in this order: (a) the total number of seasonal SKUs, (b) the balance between SKUs for men and SKUs for women, (c) within the products for men and women, how the SKUs are to be distributed for each collection (see the basic and fashion example above), (d) the respective size of the three different "launches" of the fashion line, and finally, (e) within each single launch, the relative weight of each product category.

The number of SKUs and their allocation in different merchandise categories is the first important decision to be made. The decision will be all the more effective if one can analyze certain performance parameters of the off-season collection (the previous spring-summer, when working on the plan for the next spring-summer).

A final note about width and the need for international adaptation. Often there is a tendency to make additions to a collection specifically aimed at certain geographic markets or distribution channels. These "additions" tend to lessen control of the product range, which is why you need to

1. define in the merchandising plan the amount of SKUs to be dedicated to these customizations and their structural position (in which collection, in which product categories);
2. decide, when the phenomenon assumes larger dimensions, if it is necessary to separate the plan by geographic area, planning specifically for areas with significant volume and a greater need for personalized product ranges.

2.2   *Balancing the SKUs per price range*

The second critical aspect of merchandising is to define the distribution of the SKUs in each product category according to price segment.

The idea is simple to state but rather complex to implement. Now we shall attempt a precise definition of method on this point.

1. The first thing to consider is that the plan should not only define the ideal overall quantity, but also, and above all, the proper allocation into the price ranges of the desired positioning (which translates into more options for the client). In practice this means: (a) correctly determining the price ranges of the positioning, (b)

dividing the product range to ensure respect for the positioning.
2. This process requires analyses to be performed on each single product category. It is important to note that when you get to this level of detail, it may be useful for the company to consider the product category structure carefully: a category of "formal suits" may be too large and require division into "business suits" and "suits for special events".
3. When the ranges are defined and identified as "entry range", "core range" and "high-end", the number of SKUs for each of these ranges should be defined. A breakdown of the product line that overloads the high end, or focuses too much on the extreme ranges without adequate coverage of the central range (the "core" range) must be avoided.
4. Verification of the brand's true price positioning should be performed every season. This verification will compare, in this order: (a) the desired positioning, (b) the distribution of the products in relation to the selected positioning ranges, (c) the distribution of sales across the price ranges.
5. This verification may reveal deficiencies in the product range or indicate the need to think more about the price positioning.

There may be cases where, for example, sales do not reflect the desired positioning. In these cases there will be an abnormal concentration of sales at the entry level rather than at the high end, resulting in the need for a thorough evaluation of the quality of the product line (it may be the result of poor fashion content) or a modification of the price positioning that may be under- or overestimated.

In other cases there may be an inconsistency between articulation of the product range and distribution of sales. In these cases there is room for improving product range efficiency by making it more consistent with actual demand.

Since the subject of price is extremely sensitive, it is better for analyses to be conducted over periods longer than just one season, especially when imbalances arise between selected positioning, product range distribution and distribution of sales. Phenomena such as these can hide structural issues and not merely seasonal errors: they must therefore be investigated with great care and for collections of both seasons (spring-summer and autumn-winter).

In addition, when the time horizon increases, it becomes possible to extend the analysis to sell-out performance, not only to sell-in, leading to increased reliability and relevance of the analysis results.

2.3 *The relationship between retail price and industrial cost of the product*

The third aspect to be considered is the ratio between the retail price and the industrial cost of the product. Two elements are critical here:

1. a proper understanding of this relationship is the key to profitability. In the fashion and design industry, in fact, overseeing and controlling the gross margin is the key to ensuring the profitability of the company and controlling the brand's price premium;
2. this "chain", when understood and well-managed, enables both the creative department and industrial and commercial management to speak the same language: it makes it possible to link retail price positioning to the cost of the variables (fabrics, manufacturing, washes and finishes) on which the creative division works.

In this sector, each step backwards from the retail price to cost involves several risks which should be considered carefully.

The company must first transform retail price positioning into a wholesale price structure consistent with the presence of a series of complex phenomena and structural constraints. We need only cite currency fluctuations or the presence of import duties in important markets to comprehend the nature of the problem.

To function correctly, we believe that several factors must be duly considered:

1. the considerable differences in the structure of retail mark-ups in different countries and channels of distribution. The mechanism of the "suggested retail price", though increasingly widespread and important, is not always sufficient to handle the problem properly;
2. potential changes in wholesale price determined by the sales structure, especially where: (a) there is a combination of market areas managed through agents and others managed through distributors, (b) the selling price to the distributor is not managed in a transparent way, and it becomes the working wholesale market price;

3. the presence of internal pricing rules that generate distortions, not present in a uniform price structure, such as: (a) the management of several different price lists (domestic and foreign price lists), (b) overly protective policies regarding price changes (e.g. very "conservative" exchange rates for price list preparation).

By working backwards from the wholesale price thus defined to the industrial cost target, it becomes necessary for management to define gross margin targets in as much detail as possible before development of the collection begins. This step also requires two remarks about method:

1. the need for the company to strictly control gross margins (or "industrial margin"). The definition of a margin target for this stage of the process is limited to the so-called "price list margin", that is, a definition of the relationship between the wholesale price structure and industrial cost targets. However, even when the collection is developed within the defined parameters, the "price list margin" will not be easily kept in line with the actual profit margin because of the influence of factors such as discounts, returns, deviations from standard production costs, currency exchange differences, and more. It is therefore essential for the company to master every detail of the relationship between actual profit margin and "price list margin". Only then can it transform profitability targets into operational objectives for the development of the product range.
2. Secondly, the definition of "price list margin" targets should be the result of sophisticated calculation so as not to merely link cost to price using a mathematical formula. Experience shows that, in reality, margins change according to product categories, collections and price ranges: a credible process must therefore seek to assign margin targets in as close accordance as possible with their final structure.

The third and last step links industrial costs to the cost of each individual factor, so as to transform positioning into a guideline for the creative division.

We have repeatedly emphasized the need for cross-functional management of the merchandising process. In this last step, where the entire chain of costs and prices receives the attention of management, feasibility is assured if all factors (retail mark-up, profit margins, costs of product components) are in line and consistent.

It also becomes evident that cost verification is not possible without adequate forecasting of volumes; the fact that production occurs so far in advance makes this more complicated, but it is indispensable for the correct functioning of the process.

3. The role of the merchandiser

The role of the merchandiser does not have only one definition in the fashion and design field. In many companies the role does not exist; in the organizations where it does, his/her duties can vary significantly. In this paper, rather than claiming he/she "must be present" in the organizational chart, we list some general indications of the main duties and responsibilities that the position requires.

3.1 *Structural notes*

The merchandiser links the design and product development division with marketing, sales and production divisions.

First it must ensure the link between all components of the collection - breadth, depth, range, price range.

Second, the merchandiser must liaise with marketing and sales and exchange ideas about price positioning, retail mark-up in different countries and through different channels, as well as about the timings of delivery of the collection, which also vary greatly in different geographic areas.

Third, dialogue is required with the production division which must find consistency in the merchandising plan between production decisions and expected volumes, as well as between production needs and the timing of product development, sales planning and delivery to clients.

Obviously, these connections can be made more or less effectively according to the position in the organization of the merchandiser. Without trying to dictate rules, it should be noted that the most successful results obtained indicate two possible alternatives:

1. Merchandiser reports to the General Manager or the Business Unit Manager;
2. Merchandiser reports to head of product development division.

The second alternative seems the most appropriate in situations where roles and tasks are well-established and certain tools have been perfected.

The creation of the role may however require a kind of "protection" from top management to overcome the difficulties which might arise at the beginning of this different way of working. It should be stressed that at the start of the process an investment of time and attention from the entire company will be required. Two examples demonstrate the point: the demand for very early forecasting of sales from the sales division, and the presentation of the plan to the licensor with whom an important part of the development of the collection is "negotiated".

Whatever organizational position is chosen, it is best if the merchandiser works on only one brand and, better still, only one brand line (the jeans line, rather than the "bridge" or the "first line"), especially if the business is internationally developed. The success of the merchandiser is in fact strongly linked to an in-depth and up-to-date knowledge of the business and the way the competition is distributed.

3.2   *The role of the merchandiser: duties*

The main tasks to be assigned to a merchandiser extend in three directions.

1. *Preparation and updating of the merchandising plan.*
   Managing the plan and all the information tools it requires is certainly the main task of the merchandiser. In addition to the part of the job that deals with quantification, he/she will have to work on two functional activities that require external commitment: the management of the database of the sell-out, not just of the sell-in, and discussion of the plan developed by the company with the licensor.
   These activities, as well as the one mentioned in the next step (competitive analysis support), give an externally-oriented profile to the merchandiser; it is believed that only in this way his/her value to the company is maximized. These activities emphasize the need for collaboration with the marketing and sales divisions; the duties of each should be clearly established so that the company benefits from inter-divisional collaboration without any misunderstandings and conflicts.
   As we have said, an effective management of the plan requires a

full command of the mark-up grid, namely the relationship between retail price and cost components of the product; updating and managing this information (first estimated, then verified) is part of the role of the merchandiser.

2. *Competitive analysis support*

There is no need to stress the importance in business of adequate analysis and monitoring of the competitive environment. The merchandiser has the duties and the need to continuously evaluate the positioning and the competitive strategy of the brand in relation to its competitors. The merchandiser can be used in an ideal way for monitoring activities that require important technical background such as the analysis of the price positioning/channels of main competitors.

Proper verification of the price positioning, in fact, requires a careful evaluation of the content of the product which, in many cases, the sales division can perform only to a small degree. The support of the merchandiser can thus ensure that more complete and reliable information is gathered for interpretation.

3. *Participation in sales*

Finally, a third area of the merchandiser's duties can be identified in sales support for "special" clients. The merchandiser is by definition welcome in the showroom of agents and distributors and it is important for him/her to see how the purchasing process takes place, and it is also important to verify that presentation to the client reflects the established criteria for the product design.

However, for two categories of client, the support of the merchandiser becomes crucial: for "retail" clients, (all those who dedicate space to the brand, whether it be in a single-brand shop or a "shop in shop") and for "special" clients (e.g. "mail order") who purchase restricted ranges in great depth or require tailor-made products rather than "carrying over" products from previous seasons.

The retail client should be assisted, in fact, before the sale, in preparing the merchandising space dedicated to the brand. Companies that have grown increasingly retail-oriented over time have also developed special divisions dedicated specifically to these issues. For companies in the initial stage of this process or having a limited share of their business handled in this manner, the support of the merchandiser can prove valuable.

The special client, however, does not only need additional sales service, but also a whole range of information concerning production feasibility, production testing and logistics, that are well suited to the role and duties of the merchandiser.

3.3   *The role of the merchandiser: skills*

What are the skills of a good merchandiser? We shall try to answer this question by trying to assign clear priorities:

1. First, it is an important figure with cross-functional liaison duties, and aside from the technical skills that are listed below, it is necessary for the merchandiser to have excellent interpersonal skills. The merchandiser defines the commercial strategy of the product range, in collaboration with top management, and as a result, he/she asks the right questions and guides the team to respond effectively and on time, without trying to "dictate" solutions. This is why the behavioral variable plays an important role.

2. As far as technical skills are concerned, he/she is a person who:
   - though not a fashion designer, understands and keeps abreast of trends in fashion;
   - knows the timing and methods of product development (crucial for intervening at the right moment of the process) both in the parent company and in that of any licensees involved;
   - has a wealth of technical knowledge that leads him/her to know the sources of production and their characteristics (quality requirements, production minimums and associated penalties for non-compliance, timing, costs);
   - visits distributors and agents to continually update his/her familiarity with the main commercial partners of the company and to update his/her knowledge of the market in terms of consumer and trade habits as well as what the job itself requires. He/she monitors the sales campaign and for special clients is actively involved;
   - has a market presence which makes it possible to be up-to-date on the strategies, pricing and the channels of chief competitors.

He/she possesses wide-ranging skills acquired through experience in the industry and in the world of business. The critical nature of his/her role indicates the need to nurture younger professionals who in time can occupy this role with the necessary expertise.

4. The merchandising tool

For a more complete understanding of this tool (or instrument), we give detailed examples of its implementation at crucial stages.

4.1 The definition of the product hierarchy

A good plan must reflect the strategic approach of the company. For this purpose it is essential to define the hierarchy of the product.

This figure illustrates the structure of CK Calvin Klein Jeans, the world's leading brand of "designer" jeans at the beginning of the 2000s. The correct identification of the product hierarchy shows how effective project interventions are possible only with a top-down approach.

In a situation which needs to be rationalized, for example, before defining the SKUs for a product category, it is much more effective to determine whether it makes sense to separate the basic NOOS collection

Figure 1 Product hierarchy.

	SKUs definition and allocation	
Brand / season	⟹	CK Calvin Klein jeans
Collection	⟹	CK Calvin Klein Khakis

Note: can be a flash, a delivery package, an injection, ...		CK Calvin Klein jeans
		• basic n.o.o.s.
		• fashion
		  – delivery 1
		  – delivery 2
		  – delivery 3

Gender	⟹	Man / Woman
Classification and price range	⟹	pant / 5pkt / skirt / sweater / shirt knit / jacket / accessory / etc.
Fabric	⟹	by classification
Colour	⟹	or wash for denim jeans wear
Fit	⟹	or "body"
Style	⟹	e.g. 3 bottons / brest vs single / button vs zip
Drop / length	⟹	2 - 3 - 4 - 5
Size	⟹	...

(never out of stock) from the fashion collection, or whether it is useful to articulate the fashion collection in three delivery packages or some other lesser number.

4.2 The quantification of SKUs and their distribution

The quantification of SKUs in a collection is of utmost importance. Analyses like the one below help define this important number.

The table above shows how the structure of the collection shows considerable inefficiency, in that 40% of SKUs initially ordered were cancelled during the sell-in.

The same collection also proved to be poorly balanced in the relationship between the distribution of the SKUs and the distribution of sales in the men's and women's collection.

This type of analysis, performed in as detailed a manner possible, indicates the quantification and distribution of the product range.

Figure 2 The structure of the collection: a comparison of the original proposal and the items produced

	Sales	% Sales	Initial styles	SKUs	SKUs %	Production		% Production/initial	
						styles	SKUs	styles	SKUs
Mens collection									
pants	111,752	36%	78	516		54	252	69%	49%
shirts	16,005	5%	32	173		21	73	66%	42%
jackets	16,518	5%	42	226		23	84	55%	37%
knits	123,852	39%	69	499		54	366	78%	73%
sweaters	41,742	13%	33	208		26	151	79%	73%
accessories	4,071	1%	11	47		8	25	73%	53%
Total	313,940	100%	265	1,669	48.2%	186	951	70%	57%
Womens collection									
pants	206,837	32%	87	359		66	229	76%	64%
skirts	36,466	6%	40	158		27	95	68%	60%
jackets	37,021	6%	48	197		31	91	65%	46%
shirts	43,397	7%	36	182		24	100	67%	55%
dresses	0	0%	3	9		0	0	0%	0%
knits	285,791	44%	89	630		74	470	83%	75%
sweaters	42,577	7%	48	239		40	140	83%	59%
accessories	319	0%	7	21		4	6	57%	29%
Total	652,408	100%	358	1,795	51.8%	266	1,131	74%	63%
Grand total	966,348		623	3,464	100%	452	2,082	73%	60%

With regard to the first figure (high number of cancellations) the analysis should regard parameters of gender (men's or women's), collection (basic or fashion in this case), product categories and price range. It may be discovered that the cancellations are concentrated in one of these areas, thus giving a clear indication of where to rethink the product range.

Once again there is a need to use top-down logic, as we have frequently noted.

4.3 From retail price to the manufacturing cost of the product

The planning process is even more effective when one builds a clear relationship between the projected manufacturing cost of the product and its retail price. Starting from the positioning chosen for the brand, the plan works backwards, retracing all the steps needed to transform this strategic element into operational guidelines for the creative area such as:

1. Maximum cost of materials,
2. Quality level of production,
3. Maximum cost of finishing.

For each product category in each price range.

Figure 3 From the suggested retail price to the cost of the product

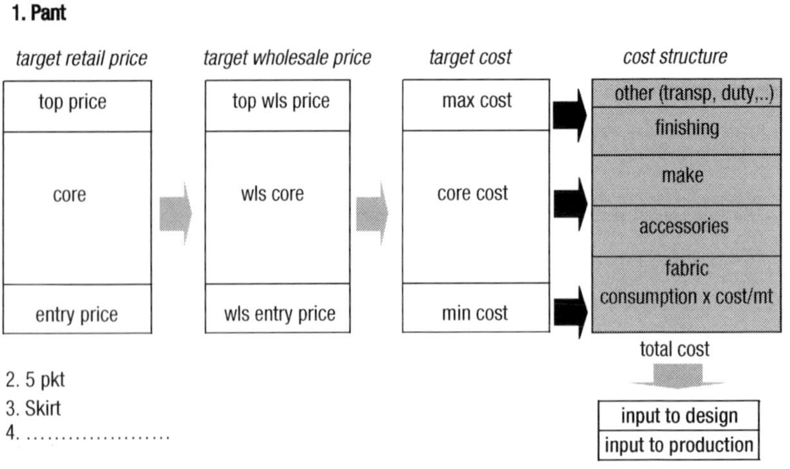

1. Pant

target retail price	target wholesale price	target cost	cost structure
top price	top wls price	max cost	other (transp, duty,...)
			finishing
core	wls core	core cost	make
			accessories
			fabric consumption x cost/mt
entry price	wls entry price	min cost	
			total cost
			input to design
			input to production

2. 5 pkt
3. Skirt
4. ....

This is not a simple exercise and should take into account a number of elements described in previous paragraphs (see "The process and the main problems ...", paragraph 2). However, it is evident that the failure to identify these structural elements will cause the pricing strategy (or the ability to achieve the desired gross margin) to be determined by the fashion and product development division, with all the risks that involves.

On the contrary, a project undertaken in an efficient and correct manner makes the task of pricing simple and free from painful last-minute adjustments when the collection is already ready for sale.

The figure shows how the task should be performed at the level of product category and price range. Where plans are being implemented, the allocation of the SKUs in every product category and price range must also be adequately specified.

Proper allocation helps give the right balance to the product range (and to profitability), thereby guaranteeing that the retail client has an adequate level of product choice which can be presented correctly to the consumer.

7 The Activities of the Collection Development Process and their Critical Aspects

by *Flavio Sciuccati and Paola Varacca Capello*

1. Managing complexity: planning

The most delicate aspects of managing collection development are planning, industrialization and management of variety, already introduced in Chapter 3. Here we will examine the effects and possible solutions of the inefficiencies that may arise in each of these processes. Fashion companies have always used their experience to manage the activities of the development process and are used to pressing schedules, unforeseen events and urgent requests. The problem is to move from common practices, often linked to personal knowledge, to formalized and objective tools that make processes more efficient (Sciuccati & Tanaka, 1997; Sciuccati & Varacca Capello, 1999). For example, the interfunctional teams adopted in some companies, with well-defined and precise moments of interaction, are an important step towards greater rationality of the process and systematic management of the problems of single areas.

At times a culture of true project management is lacking in fashion companies (Kerzner, 2013), to efficiently define the performance of activities. In other cases, companies have the tools and operational mechanisms that in theory are necessary (calendars, Gantt diagrams, various forms, collection plans, other operating plans, meetings) but then they are not respected or applied in the proper manner. Box 1 presents an example of those problems, with regard to a leather goods brand that entered the clothing world.

The intensification of competition has driven companies to develop managerial skills linked to the various management processes, but has also led to tighter schedules and other factors of complexity (described in

Box 1. The clothing collection development process

The company's creative process starts with a general meeting of the Style office, which informally outlines the trends that will form the basis for the collection guidelines. In this meeting the provisional release dates are also set. There are discordant opinions on the usefulness of this meeting. Designers, who initially thought it was useful, now consider it superfluous, thanks to the experience accumulated on the stylistic references of brands. Moreover, the meeting generally takes time away from work on the previous collection, because the Style office is often still working to manage delays and urgencies in the season being closed. The head of the Purchasing office, on the other hand, complains that the meeting is not effective, often being too "philosophical" and not making it possible to go to fairs with a precise idea of the materials required.

The concrete start of the development of the collections takes place with the first operational meeting that follows the general meeting and the closing of the final sales figures for the previous collection. The sales department sends the data to the Style office, where the secretaries produce a summary of the sell-in results divided by brand, type of material/product, model and fabric/color combination. Before this meeting, the Planning director obtains the sell-out data for directly operated stores from the sales department along with other qualitative information to interpret the final sales figures. The preparation of the data is laborious because the collections are very broad. This meeting takes place within two weeks of the presentation of the previous collection and leads to additional meetings in the next week, dedicated to brands, with the Planning director, the designers, the collection secretaries and the product assistants. In those meetings the final figures for the concluded season are discussed and the collection plan, color plan and materials plan are prepared; the final output is the collection calendar.

The Style office believes that the creative liberty of the designers must prevail, and sees the company as a laboratory for innovation. The result is that the collection presented is sometimes far from the goals of the collection plan; a collection was once redone completely ten days before presentation.

The Planning director admits that, despite his repeated efforts, he is not able to make a true plan correspond to the collection calendar. Scheduling certain activities and ensuring respect for deadlines seems impossible with the creative personnel. The calendar is adjusted continuously. In his view, a strict schedule would allow for better balancing the workloads in some sectors, like pattern making, that are insufficiently staffed compared to the volume of different models to be produced.

A final test with the models ratifies the final architecture of the collection. Afterwards the production order is launched for the fashion show garments and for the samples. The laboratory produces all of the garments and sends the finished products to warehouse. The sales prices are set in a subsequent meeting with the sales director, the compliance manager and a member of the administration office.

> An analysis begins of a proposed price list drawn up by the compliance manager based on the product costs, to which the sales director proposes adjustments as a function of market needs. Once the Italy price list has been defined, the sales director develops the international price lists based on a preset reference market for each geographic area (such as Italy for Europe), attempting to ensure the same margin for distribution by appropriately varying the sell-out prices.
> The only complete sample set for the various brands is available in the Milan showroom, since there are many items (approximately 250 models, for a total of approximately 600 articles). There are about one hundred fashion show garments (20% are for image promotion and do not enter production). The collection is presented at a fashion show in the Milan showroom, after which sales begin. Some last-minute alterations are made in production to ensure the ability to package the products, due to delays in the previous phases and the inadequate attention previously paid to the industrialization of the product.

Chapter 1), that have increased requests. Planning is therefore a critical activity, in order to define all of the activities that must be carried out within the timeframes set by the numerous people (or entities outside of the company) that revolve around the process.

By way of example, we present the Gantt charts relating to the design of a knitwear collection (Figure 1) and the activity of a style office (Figure 2), as well as a calendar of a men's clothing collection (Figure 3). With reference to Figure 1 we stress that the diagram provides KPIs for monitoring the advancement of development, with which the anticipated output and actual progress are defined.

Once the activities are correctly identified, it is important to evaluate the resulting workload, to properly measure productive capacity (essentially the person days to be allocated to the single activities). An important aspect to monitor is the level of innovation, consisting of the new fabrics to use and the new models to be developed. In this sense, we can measure the level of innovation through the percentage of new fabrics out of the total fabrics in the collection, and the new models out of the total models. Another important aspect is given by the number of prototypes that historically have been created to make it to the final collection (See Figure 6 in Chapter 3). In fact, fashion companies develop a certain number of prototypes that are then abandoned in the editing phase. In this case as well, an indicator can be calculated, represented by the final number of prototypes developed.

Figure 1 Gantt diagram of planning activities of a knitwear collection

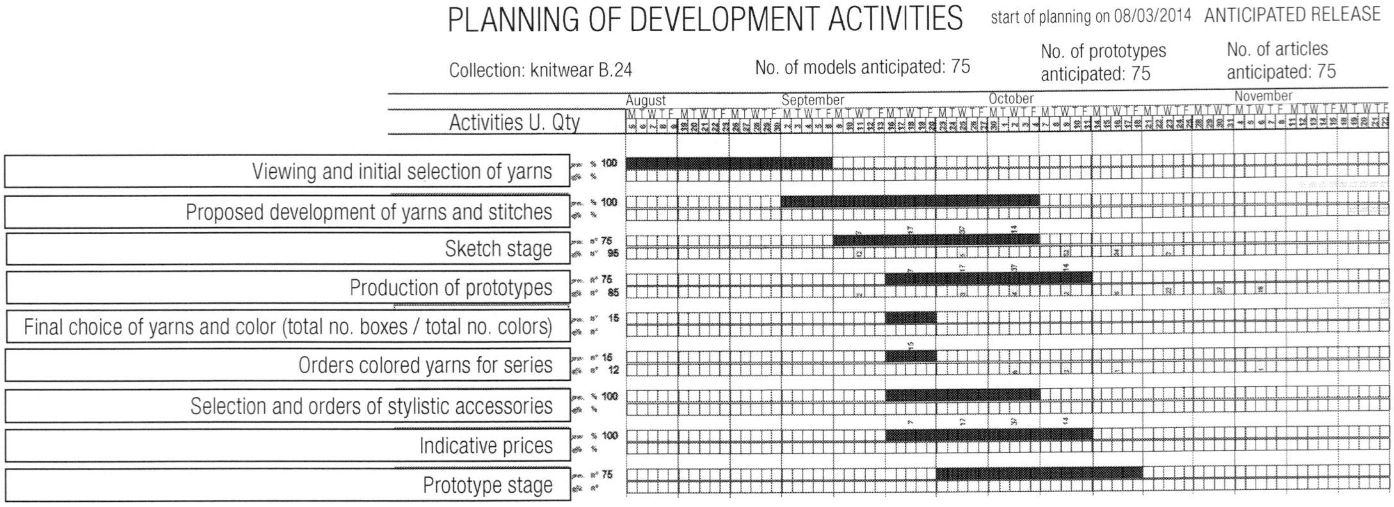

Source: prepared by Flavio Sciuccati.

Figure 2 Gantt diagram of style office activities

	Description	Weeks																
		W-4	W-3	W-2	W-1	W0	W1	W1	W1	W1	W1	W1	W1	W1	W10	W11	W12	W13	W14
1	Meeting with Paris marketing to discuss Merchandising Plan	♦																	
	Actual times																		
2	Presentation of Merchandising Plan		♦																
	Actual times																		
3	Meeting to select materials and colors			♦															
	Actual times																		
4	Entry of data in materials and colors selection gallery					■													
	Actual times																		
5	Orders of materials for Proto 1 + Proto 2					■													
	Actual times																		
6	Pre-purchases for sample collection (leather and fabrics)						■												
	Actual times																		
7	Sketch stage and data in gallery						■												
	Actual times																		
8	T&A presentation							♦											
	Actual times																		
9	Follow-up on collections meeting (round table 1)							♦											
	Actual times																		
10	Development and presentation Proto 1							■■											
	Actual times																		

Source: prepared by Flavio Sciuccati.

If to these measurements we add the quantification of the times necessary to develop the models (that vary based on the type of garment or accessory) and the timeframes required for the adjustment of the prototypes (how many times garments must generally be reworked following tests with models) we obtain a general indication of the times and resources to be involved. Time and people are obviously important resources, that are interrelated: when a company has more personnel for one or more phases of work, the overall times for collection development can be reduced even considerably, given that some activities can be carried out simultaneously. This is particularly important for activities that are found along the "critical path" of the collection that determines the actual time to market. In fashion, it is common to fully or partially outsource phases considered either too complex (that thus require specialist skills by specific suppliers) or too costly in terms of overhead (for example in the crucial phases of pattern making and prototyping, where using third parties allows for dealing with peak work periods and guarantees flexibility).

Figure 4 represents a real example of an analysis model used by a company in the leather goods sector to quantify the resources necessary for its activities. The model is based on the structure of the collection and develops the workloads and number of people required for the two "bottleneck" departments: pattern making and prototyping. The workload is quantified based on the lines to be developed for the new seasonal collection: the new models to be launched, the two lines of the prototype development and

Figure 3 Collection calendar

Activity	Collection		Target date	
			Start	End
BRAINSTORMING trends and color palettes	S1	S2	22 jan	
Search for suppliers of new types and accessories	S1	S2	12 dec	28 feb
Launch fabric test S1-S2	S1	S2	13 jan	14 mar
Delivery fabric test S1-S2	S1	S2	27 jan	28 mar
Delivery sketches 1st part to models office + request 1st series prototypes S1	S1			28 jan
Industrialization 1st series prototypes (model paper, db,…)	S1		29 jan	04 feb
Launch of production 1st series prototypes	S1			04 feb
Milano Unica	S1	S2	12 feb	15 feb
Delivery 1st series of prototypes S1 (potential additions)	S1			18 feb
1st LIMITED OPERATIONAL (viewing 1st series prototypes)	S1	S2	19 feb	
Request 2nd series of prototypes S1 (potential additions)	S1			28 feb
1st CO-PRODUCT	S1	S2	28 feb	
Definition fabrics S1 (excluding packages)	S1			29 feb
Order rolls sample S1 (excluding packages)	S1			29 feb
Definition stylistic/technical accessories sample S1	S1			29 feb
Order stylistic/technical accessories sample S1	S1			29 feb
Definition of non-stylistic accessories sample S1 (tele, bias-Pony, sleeve head rolls…)	S1			29 feb
Order non-stylistic accessories sample S1	S1			29 feb
1st fitting fault-finding 1st tranche protypes S1	S1			29 feb

Events (brainstorming, co-product, limited operational,…)

Milestones

Source: prepared by Flavio Sciuccati.

the set-up of the new models, the samples for the press and for production. This is all translated into equivalent work days through coefficients (each new model requires 1.5 days of pattern making and 2 of prototyping) and ultimately transformed into the actual needs in terms of pattern makers and prototypers.

As can easily be seen from the numbers on the right, the company has decided to outsource the high percentage of four-fifths of his pattern making and prototyping needs for the entire season (an approach which is very common among fashion companies whose strengths are high flexibility and reactivity to market demand). The workload can be quantified in terms of new models to be launched (200) and person-work days of pattern making (1.5 for each model, i.e. 300) and prototyping (two for each prototype, i.e. 400). Two prototypes are assumed for each new model. Some prototypes will be used for the press (a single person-day of pattern

7 THE ACTIVITIES OF THE COLLECTION DEVELOPMENT PROCESS

Fig. 4: Quantification of resources for the development of the collection

Capacity	Total number	No. of days pattern making	No. of days prototyping
Number of new products			
Models LAUNCHED	200	300	400
1st Proto	200	300	400
2nd Proto	200	300	400
Printing	160	160	640
Industrial samples	128	192	384

Internal pattern makers	Required prototypers
11	25
Pattern makers	Internal proto-typers
2	5
Prototypers	Capacity outsourced
9	20
Estimated models/TOT	Estimated prot. /TOT
82%	80%

Source: prepared by Flavio Sciuccati.

making and four of prototyping), while samples for production (128) require 1.5 days of pattern making and three days of prototyping. In total, eleven pattern makers will be needed.

The analysis of the times needed for the personnel to carry out specific activities is necessary not only in the development phase of the garment itself, but can also be applied to various activities, like stylistic research and the product-manager coordination process. Figure 5 presents a simple chart indicating the times and activities, that makes it possible to evaluate how many people would be necessary if the company wished to expand the portfolio of collections or lines.

Given the critical aspects and costs linked to the development of collections, the analysis can be extended to various activities and various subjects, to come up with measurable quantitative references. For example, Figure 6 shows a real analysis of the times required to produce the prototypes in various sportswear, outerwear and leather goods companies. In addition to the averages, the analysis includes measures of variance that allow for connecting the times to various portions of the prototypes produced.

Lastly, it is useful to recall that recently, many commercial software tools have been created and placed on the market with the precise goal of supporting the planning and management activities of fashion companies.

2. Managing complexity: industrialization

Industrialization is a critical step because the preparation of the technical specifications for the industrial production of the garments, the tests on the fabrics and manufacturing processes, the development of sizes and the other activities necessary to launch production, are often neglected or incomplete during the planning phase, and thus are not ready when it is time to launch production (Bini, 2011). Detailed industrialization planning is critical to guarantee maximum quality and minimum costs, but the brevity of the product cycles and short times often lead to postponing this process. Thus production ends up solving the problems, often with its own criteria which are not exactly those of style. It may be that the garments are prepared as samples and then which and how many items are produced is decided only after the first weeks of the sales campaign. Only the personnel actually involved know the difference between the sample (prototype) that has been approved or the fashion show garment, produced by expert prototypers, and the model that will be produced industrially. In some cases the garments for the fashion show are made with special sizes (those of the models) and require a modeling change before launching industrialization.

Although it is not a general rule, companies often produce prototypes internally, especially for more complex and innovative garments (including for reasons of confidentiality) and then assign industrialization to external laboratories: they provide them all of the technical information and the so-called *capo-testimone* (a sample provided by the brand to the manufacturer), leaving the laboratories to define the details of the more technical aspects for production.

In addition to preparing the *capo-testimone*, many fashion companies have technical personnel with specific expertise who visit the production facilities to ensure that production is carried out correctly and that the required quality standards are followed. It is clear that the physical proximity of the contractors that perform the work is critical. In addition, it is common to ask these laboratories for small trial productions, to verify quality standards, especially for contractors recently added to a company's list of laboratories.

The critical nature of these aspects is also to be considered in light of the extensive outsourcing that characterizes the fashion sector in general, due to the high variety of types of garments, the continuous changes that

7 The Activities of the Collection Development Process   137

Figure 5 **Measurement of times and actions**

TIME REPORT PLANNING OFFICE

Month _____ Year _____
Name _____ Name initials _____

Contract code	Activity code	Description of activity	Day 1–31	Total hours
MEE	X	MEETINGS		
TRA	X	TRAINING		
OFF	X	OFFICE ACTIVITIES		
SUP	X	SUPPORT TO OTHER BODIES		
TRI	X	TRIPS		
SIC	X	SICKNESS		
LEA	X	LEAVE		
VAC	X	VACATION		
		Totals		

Source: compiled by Flavio Sciuccati.

are made, and the specialists that are necessary for the process. For example, if a new collection is characterized by embroidery, it will be necessary to identify laboratories able to carry out that type of work, that perhaps have never been tried previously.

Figure 6 Analysis of lead times

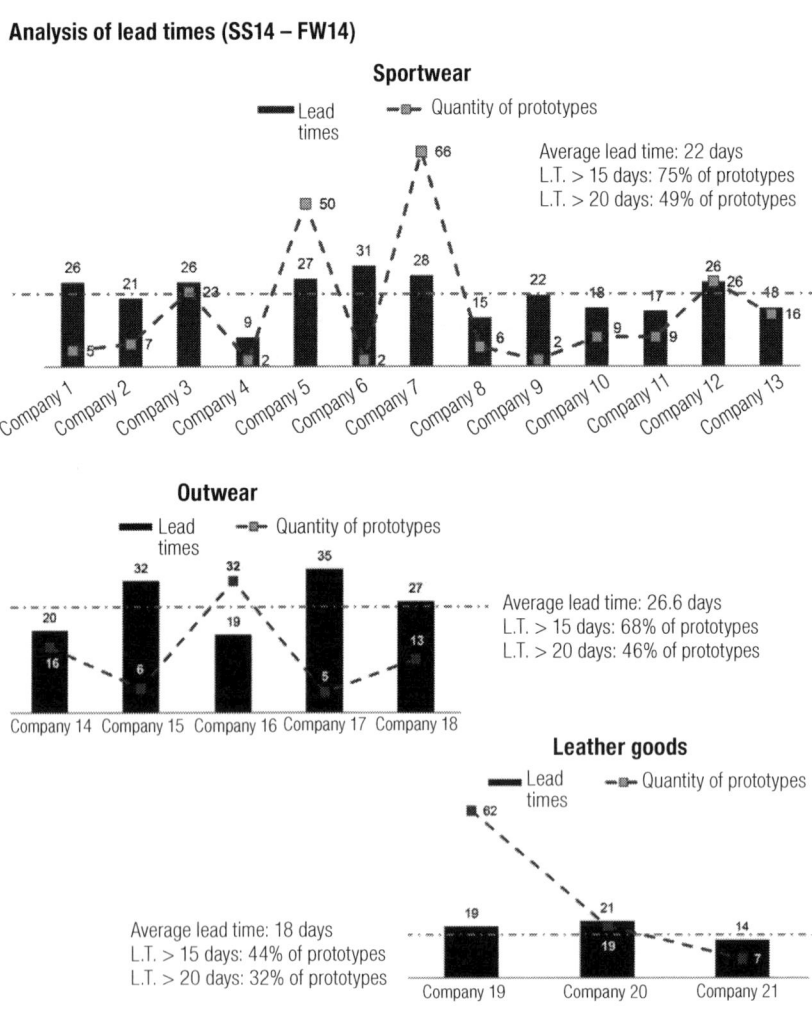

Source: prepared by Flavio Sciuccati.

3. Managing complexity: the reduction of variety

Variety is a very real problem for fashion companies, that over time have become aware of the negative consequences of collections that are too broad. In addition to the fragmentation of orders of fabrics, materials, accessories, and inefficiencies in production, such collections generate high costs of coordination and management of complexity (Cavenaghi & Secchi, 1998). There has also been recognition that excessive variety can damage a brand's sales and image. Indeed less focused collections are harder to sell, because they have a weaker stylistic identity: agents end up creating their own sample sets and the brand is weakened by an offer that is less clearly defined.

There are different approaches to reducing variety, even though it is always important for this goal to be defined by the top management and then shared inside the company. To start with, the reduction of the number of articles (type of garments), model variants and fabric variants in the sample set implies a closure toward certain categories of clients, in particular the more demanding ones who do not accept a choice between only a few offers. This in turn could lead to a loss of sales, which also needs to be compared with the real cost of a broad offer, including in organizational terms. In addition, the reduction of variety can be seen internally as a constraint on stylistic creativity and a curb on innovation of collections.

The breadth of the phenomenon of variety also extends to the phases following the definition of the collection proposal: the initial variety is modified along the way during the process, generally expanding. Aspects of additional complexity are added during the panel phase and the presentation of the collection to the sales network and the market managers (who wish to introduce particular offer elements for their markets), the presentation to special clients (who request customized versions of the collection), the collection of orders during the sales campaign (with the request for modifications and the entry of extra-collection codes for small orders of articles), and as already stated, during industrialization and production of the garments (with the introduction of modifications to the materials to improve quality or optimize working times and methods).

To manage variety, it is thus necessary to follow a structured process that begins with its measurement, goes through an evaluation of the same, and ends up with potential choices for reduction. Variety may be measured in terms of types of garments, models and variants, as in the examples in paragraph 4.2 of Chapter 5. Evaluating variety means reflecting on the consequences it produces in terms of operations and costs. In this case the analysis is harder, because those aspects do not lend themselves to an immediate evaluation, even though there are some instruments that lead to a proper approach, as we will see in paragraph 3.1. Reduction requires defining a different collection structure, with approaches that we will examine in paragraph 3.2.

3.1 *The evaluation of variety*

When the cost of a product is determined, it is possible to calculate with a good degree of precision variable costs, that derive from the materials used, the manufacturing processes and the assembly of the parts that make up the product. These costs are linked to the variety of fabrics, materials, parts (that are a consequence of the models) and the manufacturing processes themselves. The impact on costs derives from the fact that the fragmentation of production volumes over many articles causes various inefficiencies in operations:

- lower unit values in the purchase of fabrics, with the loss of economies of purchase and the emergence of problems of minimum supply quantities;
- lower unit volumes of purchases of stylistic accessories, with greater risk of excess material at the end of the season;
- reduction of the batches of models to be cut, with a resulting lower efficiency of the cutting layout and greater use of labor due to more frequent machine set-up;
- reduction of batches of finished product packages, with a drop in the yield of labor activities on the production lines and the loss of characteristics of stability and repetitiveness that a production process must have;
- increase of the possibility of error by production operators, with an increase in quality defects.

Another important cost category is the result of the difficulty to manage complexity, that entails a commitment of resources (people, above all) for the planning and monitoring of production, the procurement of materials and relationships with suppliers, the management of warehousing and shipping, and quality control along the whole process. The related costs are difficult to measure and demonstrate in relation to the increase in variety, but they can have a significant impact on fixed industrial costs.

The level of innovation of the collection, as already defined, generates personnel and materials costs in the research and development phase. In fact, the more innovative the collection, the greater the effort required: a new model requires new tests, new fabrics require arduous controls, a new accessory requires verification of matching. In addition, innovation generates a greater need for coordination between the participants in the process and possible slowdowns in development, making it more difficult to respect constraints and deadlines. Furthermore, innovation generates costs in the production phase because it requires the development of innovative production methods (or adaptation to existing methods) and the production of the technical documentation indispensable to move from the prototype to mass production. The problem gets worse in companies that outsource industrialization and production to external laboratories.

Figure 7 examines the area most impacted by variety, that of logistics-production activities. The diagram identifies on an operational level the factors that generate variety in a collection, the effects in terms of (measurable and controllable) company parameters and the resulting costs. For *fabrics*, the generators of variety are the articles and variants: the former impact the number of suppliers and production fragmentation. Having many suppliers entails diseconomies in purchasing and unreliability in terms of quality, leading to an increase of quality controls and management of procurement. Production fragmentation is caused by the need for different types of manufacturing processes (cutting, packaging, ironing and controls) in the presence of fabrics with different characteristics (for example for the design or weaving of fabric threads). This can lead to delays or errors and require additional work. The number of fabric variants implies fragmentation of the orders and an increase of anticipatory risk, since uncertain purchases are made on multiple fabrics. The result can be the cancellation of orders (if a minimum purchase level is not reached or if the variant is no longer available in the reassortment phase) or costs in terms of discounts for substitutions (provided it is possible to convince the client to select and use another fabric).

Figure 7   Effects of variety in a collection

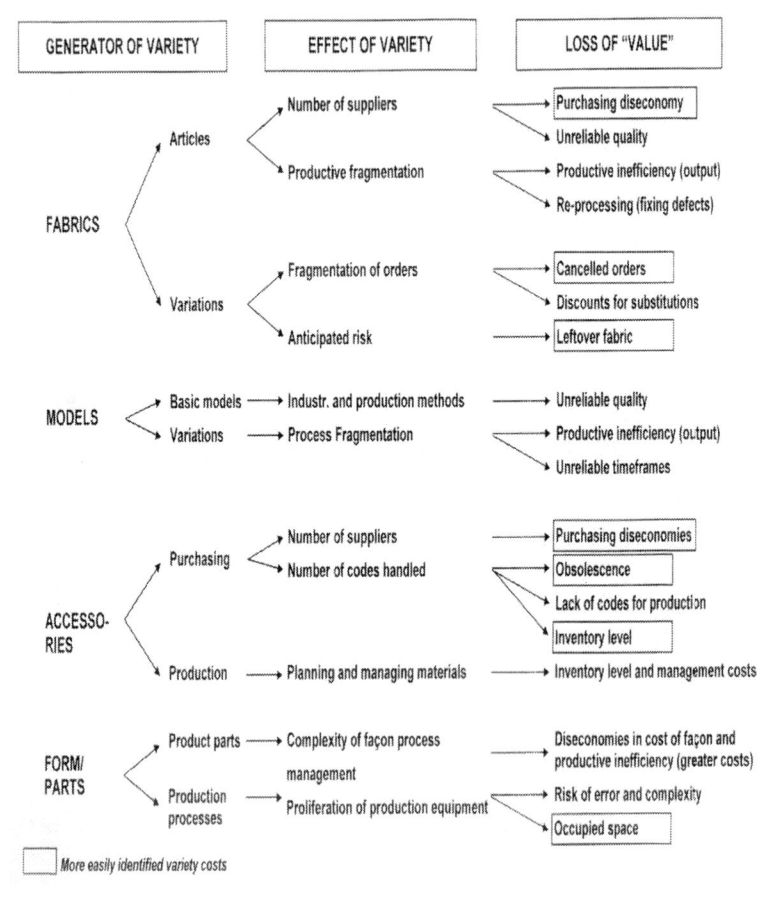

Source: Sciuccati & Varacca Capello (1999).

In the variety of *models* it is necessary to distinguish between basics and variants. The industrialization activities of the former are more onerous the more innovative the models are with respect to the previous collections. The effect of the number of variants on the fragmentation of production processes is similar to that of variants of fabrics; the effects are amplified though, when a new variant requires reviewing the method of packaging, with a consequent impact on production cycles and times.

Accessories (of style or techniques) are purchased or produced. The former have effects on the number of suppliers and create risks of obsolescence, because high numbers of codes impose purchases for multiple articles that can have high minimum orders. The level of stock will also be significant. This problem also regards product accessories, that also require careful planning to avoid empty warehouses and interruptions of production.

Shapes (i.e. the components and instruments generated by the variety of shapes and measures of which a garment consists) entail a proliferation of production tools (for example punches and markings) with inevitable impacts in terms of costs, management and space occupied. The variety of shapes also increases the complexity of manufacturing processes by external laboratories, with the result of provoking considerable diseconomies on outside production, that should be as standard and simple as possible.

Among the costs of variety and control illustrated, some are relatively easy to calculate: the weight of cancellation of orders (if the cause is reported), the stock of fabric and style materials at the end of the season and average stock levels. It is more difficult, although not impossible, to calculate all of the losses of efficiency and quality that the production system suffers due to variety, for example comparing the cost of a standard mix of variety defined at the start of the season and considered correct, with the costs of the mix actually obtained.

3.2 Methods and instruments for reducing variety

Creating awareness by the management of the problem of variety and adopting an adequate measurement system, precedes the question of how to deal with complexity and make operations more efficient. Here we will examine the VRP (Variety Reduction Program) approach, that was developed by Japanese companies in sectors in which the strong pressure for product differentiation had generated greater revenues from sales, but also a decrease of profitability, due to the increased costs of complexity (Koudate, 1991).

The basics of the methodology and goals set, principally the reduction of variety managed and the related costs, apply well to the fashion sector. For example, the Zegna group adopted the VRP concepts in collection development starting in the nineties, in a period in which the development of its network of stores had led to the emergence of the need to effectively segment the market and improve the efficiency of the operating processes.

The VRP methodology entails dealing with the issue of variety with two distinct approaches, that regard the generators of variety illustrated above (see also Figure 8):

- the top-down approach, that aims to rationalize variety by questioning the breadth of the seasonal offer starting from the products;
- the bottom-up approach, that aims to rationalize the variety of materials, accessories, processes, methods and equipment, leaving the breadth of the collection unchanged; to obtain this result, an attempt is made to standardize that which the final client does not perceive, that therefore does not have value as variety.

Working on the rationalization of the offer, the top-down approach aims to increase the efficacy of the collection, thanks to its greater characterization, and at the same time to improve efficiency of production and logistics thanks to greater economies of scale and absorption of fixed costs (especially in purchasing and production) and the economies of experience produced by less variety to manage.

On the other hand, the bottom-up approach safeguards the wealth of the offer to the final customer while rationalizing the internal constructive elements of the product following two design guidelines:

Figure 8 The "Variety Reduction Program" for the rationalization of a fashion collection

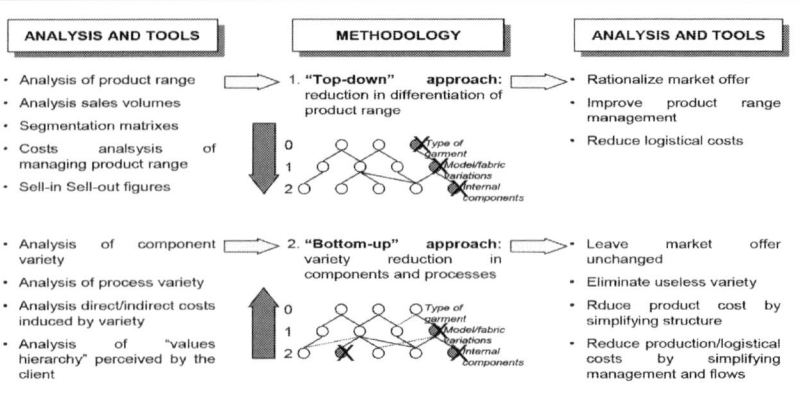

Source: Sciuccati & Varacca Capello (1999).

- the clear distinction of which components of the product are perceived by the final customer and which are not; the VRP calls the former "variable parts" (because variations increase the value of the product) and the latter "fixed parts" (to be varied as little as possible between one product and the other, or from collection to collection);
- the standardization of the fixed parts to achieve maximum operating efficiency in terms of purchase price, minimum orders, levels of stock and production batches; this concept is taken to the extreme when a material is common to all the products, or partially where rules are defined for application of one material or component with respect to another.

In a structured clothing item it is always possible to recognize the variable and fixed parts. For example, Figure 9 shows the application of the bottom-up VRP logic on a men's clothing item. The internal accessories (such as threads, shoulder pads, adhesives or reinforcements) can be standardized greatly, when the models are designed with the logic of using as much as possible what has been developed and tested. If this does not already take place at the beginning of development, a simple review of the product allows for introducing the required standardization. It is also not indispensable for external variety (sizes and measures for the shape, designs and colors for the aesthetics of the item) to translate into equal variety of the internal visible or semi-visible parts (internal lining, buttons, etc.).

The top-down approach should be taken by those companies that realize that they offer an excessive range of articles, that generate little additional value and entail problems for sales such as:

- lengthening of sales times by sales force to clients;
- risks of ad hoc personalizations by the agent/seller to satisfy its clients;
- greater difficulty of selection by distribution and thus greater risk of unsold items;
- cannibalization among the items in the collection and potential overlapping with unsold items from previous seasons.

In addition, a collection is redundant and needs a top-down reduction if its breadth generates an internal management effort that is not commensurate with the volumes and turnover generated by the single items (articles,

Figure 9 Application of the "Fixed parts" concept

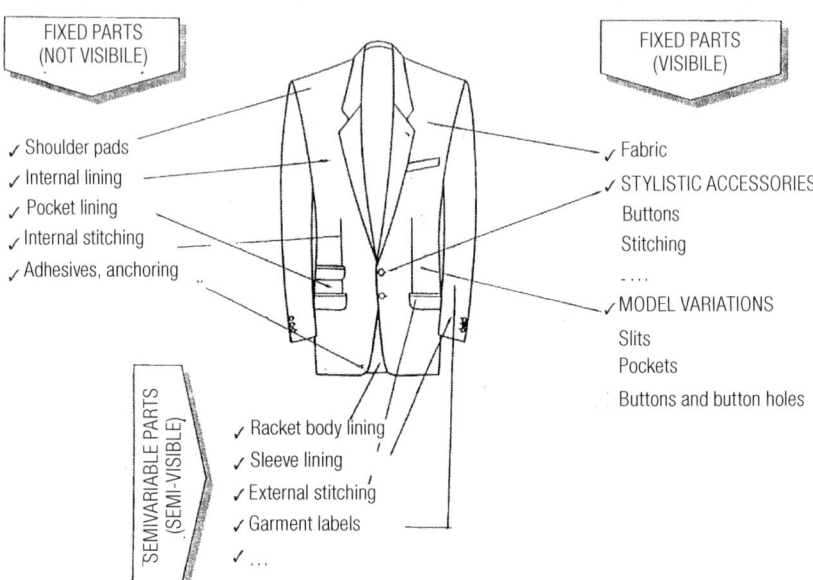

fabrics, models, accessories) and by the company's income result. There are various instruments to identify the areas of the offer to be reduced (on this point, see Chapter 5):

- the ABC analysis of volumes and turnover (by type of garment, model and fabric);
- the deviations of productivity of the articles offered with respect to the goals;
- the analysis of the unsold items of the variants offered;
- the comparison of the sell-in data for the sales campaign and the sell-out data from the stores, to evaluate the real impact on the final customer and the validity of a focused or broader offer;
- targeted interviews or focus groups with the market managers, sales network and main clients to evaluate possible areas of rationalization (redundant areas of the collection at the expense of empty areas in the offer);
- the collection of internal management data on unsold items, order cancellations, and delivery delays.

3.3 Some concrete experiences

To provide examples of what has been presented to this point, we will illustrate some concrete interventions involving evaluation and reduction of the variety of fabrics and technical accessories in the context of men's formalwear collections. The problem of variety of fabrics is very important in clothing, because at times there is a tendency to exaggerate the number of varieties offered to satisfy various types of clients, generating a series of problems, such as not reaching large quantities for each variant or accumulating stock that is hard to use. This is a typical problem in men's formalwear, because the wealth of a collection is determined principally by the fabrics.

Figure 10 illustrates an analysis of fabric variants, with reference to two men's clothing collections managed by the same company. The ABC curves express the distribution of meters sold with respect to the variants offered. Collection A has approximately 250 fabric variants with a very steep ABC curve (80% of sales are represented by 40 variants). Collection B has approximately 450 variants and the ABC curve shows a better distribution of sales. The efficiency performance of the two collections, measured in terms of meters sold per fabric variant, is similar (approximately 200 meters per variant), even though it was achieved with opposite management methods, both of which are however valid: a small number of variants (collection A) and a balanced distribution of sales per variant (B).

The two collections have different logics. A is a "fashion" or "designer" collection, and thus heavily characterized by the fabrics, of which there are few, but carefully selected variants. This collection, sold principally in showrooms, is very well-defined from a stylistic point of view. This explains the form of the ABC curve. The more traditional fabrics use fewer meters and are included to satisfy particular clients. B is a collection with an industrial brand, aimed at differentiated customer segments, and meets needs that are also different in geographic terms (tastes and climates). The high number of fabric variants is justified by the extent of the client base.

This experience represents the result of an analysis conducted in the context of a process of evaluation and reduction of variety. In the subsequent seasons the meetings for planning collection B were oriented to a more targeted segmentation of clients, and the variants were reduced by 20%. The crucial aspect of the rationalization consists of planning the varieties to be offered and being able to manage them from the time the col-

Figure 10 Interpretative model to rationalize the offer of fabrics in collections following the VRP top-down approach

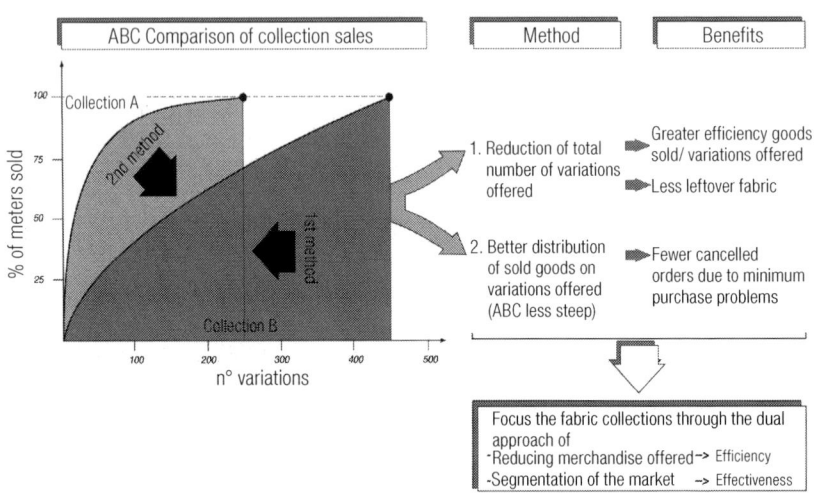

Source: Sciuccati & Varacca Capello (1999).

lection is conceived. To that end, it is necessary to assess the space which innovative articles may have and as a consequence, define the collection plan.

As we have seen, the bottom-up approach meets a need for operational and logistical efficiency that impacts variety and control costs. This approach also requires a considerable effort in terms of internal analysis, registration of the parts, accessories and manufacturing processes, collection of information from the various offices and processing of data. The instruments to be used to classify the variety determined by the product structure are:

- the reconstruction of the varieties managed in the collection, that typically are:
  - variety of accessories (distinguishing between stylistic and technical-functional);
  - variety of shapes of the product and related development tools;
  - variety of production processes (phases, parameters, times, methods skills);
  - variety of quality controls (incoming, in-process, outgoing).

- the measurement of variety (type and number of parts used) at the level of technical specifications of the product, highlighting the areas of principal variety;
- a group discussion of improvement of the variable parts and fixed parts;
- the search for the maximum standardization of fixed parts, through strict involvement of product managers and pattern makers, with potential experimentation on prototype garments or market test items.

The reduction model always takes place through a working group that brings together the key functions; style, industrialization, production and sales. The critical interlocutors change depending on the problem dealt with: designers, for example, have a crucial role for style accessories, while for technical accessories the pattern makers are asked to identify constructive solutions to use the same component in multiple garments. The components to be concentrated on are the most valuable ones, to maximize the financial benefits of reducing their number.

To summarize, the bottom-up approach is successful if success is attained in demonstrating the uselessness of certain varieties (compared to their costs) and raising awareness among the creative personnel of the need to seek efficiency. This requires considerable effort directed by the company management. A VRP project needs careful planning of activities, and the identification of a person in charge who is able to involve the structure and ensure that its personnel recognize the need to pursue the reduction process.

The applicability of a VRP approach also depends on the type of product. A bottom-up VRP is suited to products that already have a certain level of standardization (men's formalwear, outerwear) or are addressed to commercial segments of the market, where cost control needs are important. Where innovation and fashion content dominate, top-down approaches can be useful.

The possibility to rationalize variety also depends on the type of relationships that exist between design and production. The companies that operate under license can have more difficulties imposing the needs of variety reduction than those that produce with their own brands and integrate creation and production.

Bibliography

Bini, V. (2011), *La supply chain nella moda*, FrancoAngeli, Milan.
Cavenaghi, S. & Secchi, R. (1998), "Razionalizzare lo sviluppo delle collezioni. Risultati di un'indagine nel tessile-abbigliamento", *Economia & Management*, n. 3, pp. 111-126.
Kerzner, H.R. (2013), *Project management: a systems approach to planning, scheduling, and controlling*. John Wiley & Sons, New York (NY).
Koudate, A. (1991), *Il management della progettazione*, ISEDI, Milan.
Sciuccati, F.M. & Tanaka, M. (1997), Riprogettare il sistema di produzione. Quality, cost, delivery: i tre pilasti della competititivà, Edizione Il Sole 24 Ore, Milan.
Sciuccati, F.M. & Varacca Capello, P. (1999), "Il sistema moda e la gestione della varietà", *Economia & Management*, 5, pp. 57-72.

The Authors

Giorgio Brandazza has been CEO of the Elie Saab Group since 2013. He has acted as a senior manager or consultant in various companies in the fashion sector in both Italy and abroad, including Gft Group, Legler–Polli Group, Fingen Group (ck Calvin Klein Jeans and Guess Jeans) and Boggi. He is SDA Bocconi Professor in the area of Strategy and Entrepreneurship. He was the co-director, and is currently a Lecturer at Mafed (Master in Fashion, Experience and Design) at SDA Bocconi School of Management. He is also a lecturer for the LBM (Luxury Business Management) track of the MBA at SDA Bocconi, on the issues of merchandising and retail merchandising.

Nicola Misani is a Researcher in Management in the Department of Management and Technology of Bocconi University. His area of research includes business strategy, sustainability, corporate social responsibility and the management of multinational companies. He collaborated on the annual Fashion and Luxury Insight report published by SDA Bocconi School of Management and *Altagamma*. His research has been published in various international journals, including: *Journal of Business Ethics, Scandinavian Journal of Management, Business Strategy and the Environment, Business Ethics: A European Review, Ecological Economics, Journal of World Business*, and *International Business Review*.

Davide Ravasi received his PhD in Business Administration from Bocconi University of Milan. He is currently Professor of Strategic and Entrepreneurial Management at Cass Business School, London, where he directs the PhD program in Management. He is interested in the cultural processes that influence the genesis and spreading of new objects and practices, and their adoption by individuals and organizations. His research has been published in various academic journals, such as: *Administrative Science Quarterly, Academy of Management Journal, Organization Science, Journal of Management Studies, Journal of Business Venturing, Industrial and Corporate Change* and *Organizational Dynamics*.

Diego Rinallo, Ph.D., is Associate Professor of Marketing and Consumer Culture at Kedge Business School (Marseilles) and affiliate researcher CERMES - Center for Research on Marketing and Services at Bocconi University. He is a faculty member of the Milano Fashion Institute and Maison Mediterranéenne des Métiers de la Mode. Over the years he has conducted numerous studies on fashion, often with a critical view and focusing on the unwelcome effects on the environment, society and consumers. He is the author of *Trade Shows in the Globalizing Knowledge Economy* (Oxford University Press, 2014) and *Event Marketing* (Egea, 2011), in addition to many research articles in journals such as: *Journal of Marketing, Journal of Business Ethics, Economic Geography, Industrial Marketing Management* and *Journal of Business Research*. He is a member of the editorial board of the *Journal of Global Fashion Marketing*.

Flavio Sciuccati is Senior Partner at The European House-Ambrosetti, where he is responsible for the Industry, Organization and Value area and the point of reference for the Textile, Fashion and Luxury sectors (in 2009 he founded the group's Global Fashion Unit). Sciuccati holds a degree in Nuclear Physics, as well as an Executive MBA from SDA Bocconi (with which he collaborates), and is active in consulting on issues of product development, operations and supply chain management at the international level. He has been a Lecturer on Technology Management and Competition at Bocconi University and is the author of the book *Riprogettare il Sistema di Produzione* (Edizioni Il Sole 24 Ore).

Paola Varacca Capello is Lecturer in Management in the Department of Management and Technology of Bocconi University, where she graduated and currently teaches Business Administration and Management of Fashion Companies. She is SDA Bocconi Lecturer for Mafed (Master in Fashion, Experience and Design) on the issue of product development and merchandising. She is a Lecturer and member of the academic committee of the Milano Fashion Institute. She has published various books, articles and case studies on fashion, luxury and jewelry, and collaborated on the preparation of the annual Fashion and Luxury Insight report published by SDA Bocconi and Altagamma.